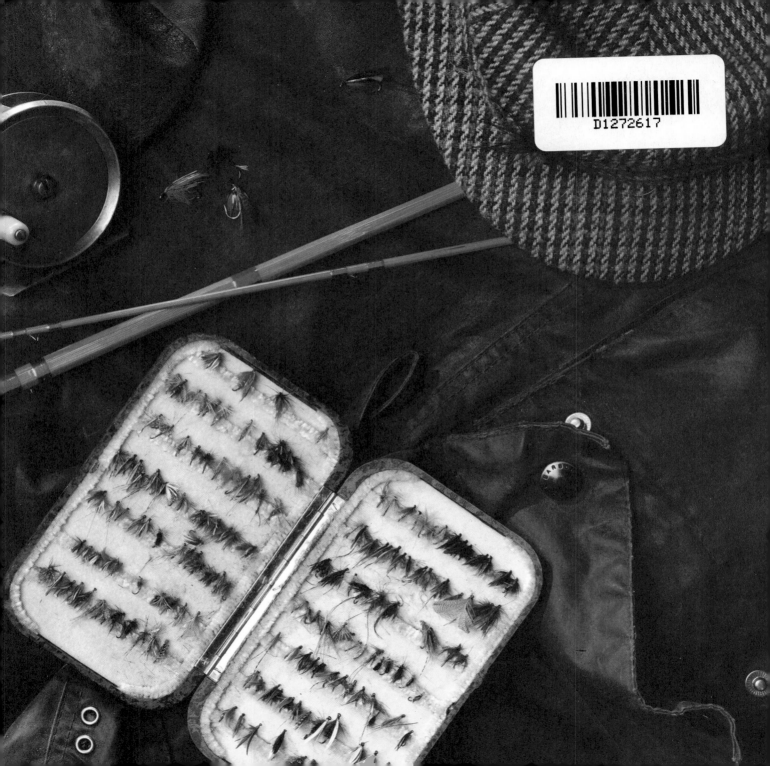

D1272617

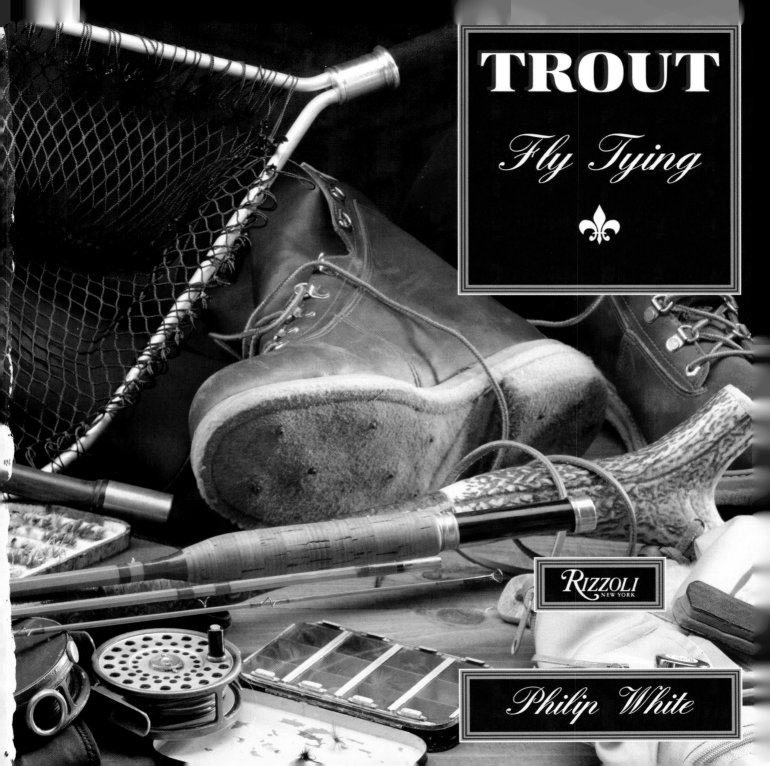

TROUT

Fly Tying

RIZZOLI
NEW YORK

Philip White

First published in the United States of America in 1995
by RIZZOLI INTERNATIONAL PUBLICATIONS INC.
300 Park Avenue South, New York, NY 10010

© 1994   Copyright Harlaxton Publishing Limited
© 1994   Copyright design Harlaxton Publishing Limited

All rights reserved. No part of this work may be reproduced
in any manner whatsoever without permission in writing from
Rizzoli International Publications, Inc.

Publisher: Robin Burgess
Design & Publishing Manager: Rachel Rush
Cover Photography: Chris Allen, Forum Advertising Limited
Editor: John Wilshaw
Illustrator(s):   Linden Artists
Photography: Chris Allen, Forum Advertising Limited
Typesetting: Seller's, Grantham
Colour separation: GA Graphics, Stamford
Produced: Imago, Singapore
Title: TROUT Fly Fishing
ISBN: 0-8478-1868-3
LC: 94-41900

Some of the flies described in this book originated in excess of a hundred years ago. They have withstood the test of time, technology, and "anglers myth" to remain as effective today as they have ever been.

For authenticity, the fly tying materials used are to the original and traditional recipes. These naturally occurring materials were originally chosen for their known behaviour and colouration when emersed in the water, and proven effectiveness over many years of subsequent use.

In certain countries, alternative or synthetic materials may be substituted if the original materials are not available.

Contents

Preface

Some say that the ability to fish is a sure sign of a badly spent youth. True or false, I was never out of water as a boy, cold when playing in it and very often a good deal warmer when I got home soaking!

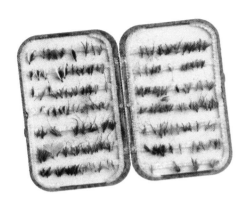

Flies ancient and modern.

I knew the whereabouts of every frog pond for miles and spent days constructing dams across streams at least two feet wide and six inches deep. Sadly, these days youngsters with a wanderlust cannot be let out of sight, never mind miles away from home, but that's progress.

By 12 years of age I was rarely without a rod, cycling the three miles to the river. Then I discovered fly fishing.

Whenever my elder brother was not watching, I pinched his rod and was off in search of dace and grayling. Seeing my enthusiasm, an old chap gave me a couple of old greenheart salmon rods and some fishing books.

I cannibalised those old rods into trout rods and wore out my thumb reading those books. I drank in every word.

One book had a chapter about fly dressing and my life was ruined. I became a compulsive fly dresser. Feathers were plucked out of pillows and I haunted poulterers' shops for game bird feathers.

I dressed those flies in my fingers, but then birds of a very different feather took my fancy and all was forgotten for a few years. Happily, commonsense prevailed and I was soon back to a far more enjoyable kind of vice.

Eight lessons later by Fly Dressers Guild founder Don Haynes and I was firmly hooked for life, discovering skills I never thought I even possessed. My mind numbing office job left behind, I landed a river keeper's job on the River Avon in the south east of England at the ripe old age of thirty-one.

I was assured that, because I knew absolutely nothing about the job, I would quickly adapt to the way the owner wanted the river run. In those days, the river was one of the very first fully managed and stocked artificial trout fishery.

Fly reels of yesteryear.

After an interlude at a private club water in Sussex, I moved to my present job as head river keeper to the Duke of Rutland on his Haddon Hall estate in Derbyshire, being responsible for 13 miles of double-bank dry fly fishing on the Derbyshire Wye and its tributaries, all favourite haunts of Izaac Walton and Charles Cotton.

My fly tying has led me to Germany, Holland and more recently to America as well as demonstrating at the British fly shows and game fairs.

Now, with countless trout and almost as many lost flies behind me, my greatest pleasure of all is to see the grin on a beginner's face after taking his first trout on a fly of his own making. Truly a magical moment never to be forgotten.

Above: Head river keeper, Philip White.

Introduction

Why, with so many books already written about fly fishing and fly tying, was I asked to produce yet another one ?

It was not because I am an expert, for I believe that there is no such thing. More likely it was because I can still remember vividly the multitude of things I badly needed to know about after picking up my first fly rod.

Although my whole life has been a matter of flies, feathers, trout and trout fishers, I am at best, what I rate as an experienced beginner. In fact, there is more to learn about the trout fishing game than can possibly be learned in a single lifetime.

I have included a little history and have approached the fly tying aspect by assuming a total lack of knowledge. The many books I read when I started always lost me somewhere along the line, simply because they blindly assumed I knew what they were talking about.

A London-mode fly reel.

So, rather than attempt a complete pattern guide, I have dwelled more on fly dressing methods and techniques. This is the way I teach, and it seems to work.

Nobody can know it all and the greatest pleasure in fly dressing is to be with a group of like-minded people of all abilities swapping techniques and new ideas, comparing materials or fly styles or, dare I say it, just talking. Maybe a few more politicians should try it!

Opposite: The fly dressers' bench.

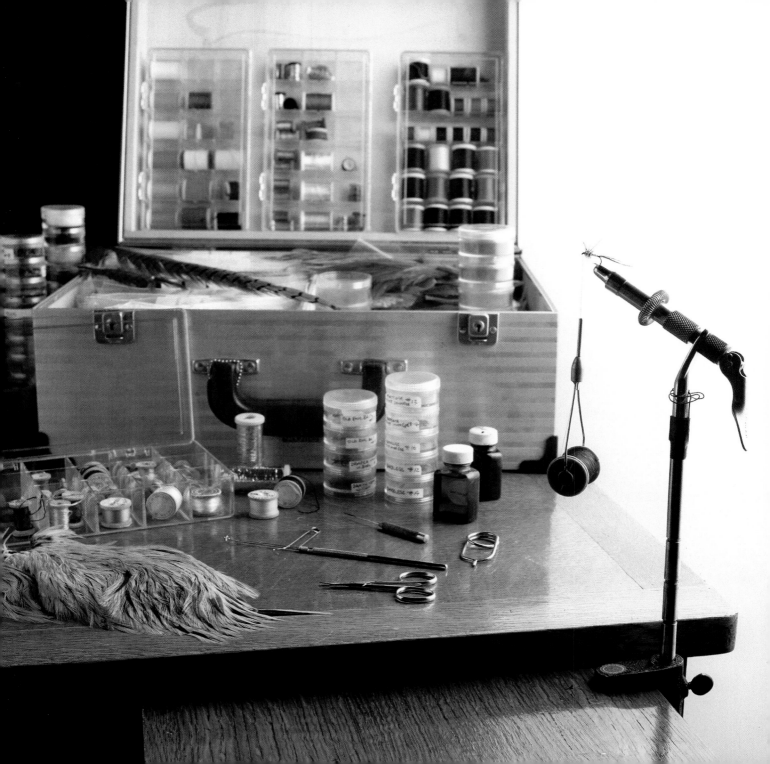

In the beginning

"They fasten red wool around a hook and fix to the wool two feathers that grow under a cock's wattles and which colour is like wax."

So it all began when in AD 200, Claudius Aelian related what he had seen after watching Macedonians fishing the River Atraeus. This was the first ever mention of fly fishing and quite a departure from the usual way of catching fish with spears, nets or traps.

Little more was heard about fishing with an artificial fly for another 1000 years and more until 1496, when dressings for a dozen flies were revealed in the famous Book of St Albans, a work dealing with hunting, hawking and all matters of knightly interest.

The book, published by one Wykyn de Worde and generally attributed to Dame Julyans Berners, Prioress of Sopwell Nunnery, also provides a calendar of the flies to use in the different months.

The fly for March, a simple affair thought to represent the March Brown, and easily tied on a modern size 12 hook without a vice, was described as a "donne fly of the donne wool and wyngis of a petryche."

I can easily say that "donne" means the mousy brown colour we know today as dun and that the "wyngis of a petryche" is simply that the wings are made from the wing feather of an English partridge. Or does it mean that the wings are made of partridge body feathers or from the tail feather? We will never know, but flies dressed with all the permutations always look good.

This fly, together with the eleven others, was repeated with little alteration for the next couple of centuries with few additions, save for John Dennys' Secrets of Angling, who in 1615, gave a new dressing for a general fly that varied in colour according to the month of the year.

In Izaac Walton's Compleat Angler, written another 40 years on, the same list is trotted out again but with two very telling remarks which have a vital bearing on the modern argument as to who invented the dry fly.

"You are to note" says Piscator "that there are twelve kinds of artificial flies made to angle with upon the top of the water. Note that the fittest season of using these, is in a blustering windy day when the waters are so troubled, that the natural fly cannot be seen, or rest upon them."

Then we are urged to "not let your line exceed, especially for three or four links next to the hook, I say not exceed three or four hairs at the most, though you may fish a little stronger above, in the upper part of your line: but if you can attain to angle with one hair, you shall have more rises and catch more fish…"

We are also told to have the sun at our face, the wind at our back and to use a short line, all of which suggests that fly fishing at this time was mainly done by dapping with floating flies.

Later editions of the Compleat Angler, printed from 1676 onwards, included the work of Charles Cotton who revealed a list of 65 flies. We really know little of the styles in which these flies were tied and it was

Above: Creating a new fly.

not until the year 1826, in a revised edition of Richard Bowlker's "The Art of Angling" written 80 years earlier, that we can see what the flies really looked like.

Before this colour illustration, the only references were woodcuts, engravings and the lucky few who saw the flies themselves.

From then to the present day, the trout fly developed in different ways wherever in the world trout were found or could be transplanted. This all took place slowly at first with some aspects being very localised.

The fish imitating patterns, such as the Matuka developed in New Zealand, and American streamers, are classic examples of local evolution being involved long before they become accepted elsewhere.

Above: Tying on the fly of the moment.

One or two free-thinking English fly dressers were working on similar lines, especially those fishing the Blagdon reservoir, the first of Britain's modern stillwater trout fisheries. They were devising small fry imitations almost as soon as the water opened in the early years of this century.

Doctor J. C. Mottram was such a pioneer and he devised patterns as imitative as anything being created at today's vices. They even used turkey marabou to suggest movement coupled with translucency. Marabou 90 years ago – is there anything really all that new?

Unfortunately, much of the work done by these pioneers was suppressed and even traditional lake flies such as the fry imitating Alexandra were banned from many waters for years.

The stocking of new English reservoirs with trout in the 60's broke down many of these stupid barriers and it was not long after the opening of Chew Valley, Grafham and Rutland Water that the brakes came off stillwater trout fly design.

The new waters suddenly made trout fishing available to the ordinary working man wherever he lived, rather than in isolated areas of the country where trout streams abound.

Traditional attitudes to the old patterns changed, and although many favourites are still with us, the speed of the development of newer and more imitative patterns has been phenomenal. Other influences upon the roller-coaster changes in fly styles are relatively cheap and fast air travel, coupled with easy access to international fly fishing literature. Today, we can all see what is happening as it happens and the ideas buzz to and fro around the world.

All sorts of things were happening on the river bank in the 70's, among them the demise of the tweed-jacketed gentleman image of the English fly fisher, his place being taken by a less formally dressed angler clad in lightweight slacks and multi-pocketed waistcoat not hidebound by tradition in either his fishing or fly dressing.

Above: An old cast box.

Evolution of the fly

"The trout is a carnivore, feeding on small fish and a host of insects that fly dressers world-wide have spent centuries attempting to imitate with fur and feather."

Trout will eat just about anything they can swallow and it is horrifying to see how large a mouthful they can cope with.

Not all trout develop this trait thank goodness, but the growth rate of those that do is quite phenomenal compared to fish that decide on a mainly insect only diet.

As the trout grows, so does its appetite, and almost all will eventually include fish in their adult fare. This diet will include snails, water beetles, all kinds of aquatic fly larvae as well as crayfish, fish and any bugs or beetles that fall into the water.

Large trout will quite happily swallow frogs, small mice and even voles that stray too far from the bank. Trout are great free-loaders too. It does not take them long to realise that if they set up home near a bridge they will be treated to all sorts of human picnic fare.

I know a fish called George. This old timer lives in the pool below my house and has grown to his stately eight pounds weight on more than his fair share of sandwiches tossed in by walkers crossing his bridge home.

George is virtually uncatchable on a fly and has avoided capture by means fair and foul over the past four years since he was last caught and moved away to a place safe from poachers.

Unfortunately, George could not bear to be away from his home under the bridge and he was back in his old haunts the following morning. Now George is even craftier, only taking a snap at a sandwich scrap after allowing his smaller brothers to sample the food for hidden dangers.

Fly dressings have been handed down from father to son, but the information for English flies first recorded in 1450; as well as those from the Leon district of Spain, their dressings written down by Juan de Bergara in 1624; and the flies of Italy's Seisa Valley, found in old church records dating back to 1760; provide a useful insight into the style of these ancient flies and the materials used to dress them.

Since two of those records have a direct religious connection, could it be that fishing had a much higher importance in those days, or is it merely that the holy orders were the only people who could write?

It is interesting to compare artificial flies from the different areas of Europe and to see the many similarities between those of 18th century Italy and the already ancient

Opposite: A Brown trout and a box of mayflies are a perfect combination.

traditional flies of England. These old patterns were usually called "Spider" flies although interestingly, they have recently re-emerged in America under the name "Soft Hackles".

All are freely based on the old dressings, especially those of English Northcountry fly fisher Pritt. The bottom line is that they are enjoying just as much success in the USA now as they did in their infancy in Europe all those years ago.

The ancient books tell us clearly that the flies were fashioned from readily available wools, feathers, furs and silks.

Charles Cotton and Izaac Walton in The Compleat Angler have this to say:

"And then an ingenious angler may walk by the river and mark what flies fall on the water that day, and catch one of them, if he sees the trouts leap at a fly of that kind; and then always having hooks well hung with him and having a bag also with him, with bear's fur, or the hair of a brown or sad-coloured heifer, hackles of a cock or capon, several coloured silk and crewel to make the body of the fly, the feathers of a drake's head, black and brown sheep's wool or hog's wool and hair, thread of gold and silver, silk of several colours, especially sad coloured, to make the fly's head: and

Above: Tying on a damsel fly imitation.

there be also other coloured feathers, both of little birds and of speckled fowl: I say, having those with him in a bag, and trying to make a fly, though he miss at first, yet shall he at last hit it better, even to such perfection that none can well teach him: and if he hit to make his fly right, and have the luck to hit also where there is a store of trouts, a dark day, and a right wind, he will

catch such a store of them, as will encourage him to grow more and more in love with the art of fly-making."

Olde English grammar maybe, but Walton's description of the contents of the fly dressers' dubbing bag and the development of his tying skills through trial and error, is little different now than when he published it way back in 1653.

these materials came on the fly dressing scene after Walton's day, when bears were more common in England than they are now, since these materials are commonplace in dressings for 19th century flies.

Strangely, while these dubbings have changed over the centuries, hackles and winging feathers seem to have had a much longer continuity since feathers from partridge and mallard are mentioned from 1496 right through to today, while hackle feathers taken from a capon are recommended by Claudius Aelianus in AD 250.

The traditional materials used in any area reflect what is readily found. If you pick up a fly dressing book from anywhere in the world you would find a list of materials reflecting local animal and bird life.

Of course, some exotic feathers from the tropics will be there too, but on the whole, these fancies are used more for salmon than trout flies. It is not just the materials, but the way they are used that is important and none more so than the dubbings. A classic illustration of their importance comes in The Compleat Angler during a conversation between Viator and Piscator.

Viat. "This dubbing is very black."

Pisc. "It appears so in the hand, but step to the door and hold it up betwixt your eye and the sun and it will appear a shining red. Let me tell you, never a man in England can discern the true colour of a dubbing in any way but that, and therefore choose always to make your flies on such a bright sunshine day as this… and be sure to make the body of your fly as slender as you can. Very good! upon my word, you have made a very handsome fly…"

A better recommendation for careful selection and use of dubbing I have yet to see. Later anglers continued this meticulous care; a glance at the fly list given by H. C. Cutliffe in 1863, for example, shows that the exact part of the body from which the fur should be taken is stipulated in many of the dressings.

Cutliffe was particularly fond of hare's flax, or guard hairs which he shaved off with a cutthroat razor. His dressings are attributed to the West of England but at the same time in the North and the Scottish borders, a different style of fly was developing with slightly different characteristics.

There, flies with plain silk bodies often sparsely dressed with fine, soft furs and hackled with soft feathers, were very fashionable. Fished downstream, the fibres of both body and hackle kicked in the current so they needed to be stiff and spiky.

Observe that he talks about wools and crewels, bear's hair, hog's wool and fur taken from a sad or, doughy-coloured heifer. Elsewhere in the book, he mentions fur taken from spaniels and greyhounds, herls from the peacock and ostrich and yet oddly, there is little use for fur from a hare, rabbit, fox cub or a squirrel.

We cannot escape the conclusion that

Northern flies were fished up and across to drift with the current, their much softer hackles responding to the water movement.

Any dubbing was sparse to allow the coloured silk to glow through to create a subtle body colour. Some of the northern flies were finished off behind the hackle to support them in the current. On the Italian Seisa, flies were tied in much the same way, the hackles put on with the concave side facing forwards instead of the more conventional way accepted almost anywhere in the world today. The reason for the about-face style was that the hackle fibres had more kick in the fierce current of the tumbling mountain rivers and made the fly look more alive.

Do not forget that fishing with a fly was not just a sport in those days but a way of feeding hungry families. The flies had to work and be made as easily and cheaply as possible.

Among these old fishers who caught trout to live was England's W. C. Stewart, who wrote the influential book The Practical Angler as well as being the designer of the highly effective Stewart style of spider flies.

Two things happened during the 19th century which affected the evolution of the

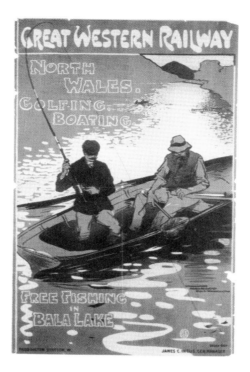

An angler fishing on a North Wales lake.

trout fly more than any other event in fly fishing history. The first was the advent of the eyed hook in the late 1800's. This discovery was attributed to H. S. Hall but was suggested before 1850 by Wheatley, coinciding with the development of the modern dry fly which soon became popular everywhere and even obligatory on the chalk streams of southern England.

Dubbed silk bodies lost in favour to feather herls and quills partly because they absorbed less water and because they helped create the slimmer, waterproof bodies much sought by those striving for exact imitation of the natural flies.

The second signpost was a sudden urge to see how the rest of the world lived. The building of railways across continents to join up with steam ships bound for all parts of the globe spurred on the "migration" of trout from the northern to the southern hemisphere as well as different species being moved across the Atlantic.

During this pioneering era, anglers from established fly fishing countries took their fly patterns to Australia and New Zealand and it is easy to see the influences of these old European flies anywhere that trout are fished with a fly.

Immediately, fly dressing development and evolution was pushing on hard, with local materials being introduced and special patterns being devised to suit particular local conditions, often as a result of seeing how the native fishermen angled for other species of fish.

It is fascinating to look at the now established patterns from these newer trout fishing countries and to see how they have influenced European fly tying.

One idea transported away from its

origins in Australia and New Zealand was the use of a simple strip of rabbit fur. American lure fishers quickly saw its potential, re-naming it the Zonker, and now few British anglers who fish the large man-made reservoirs would be without a selection of these highly mobile lures in their boxes.

There is no doubt that the development of all manner of flies and lures was largely given a kick start with the introduction of synthetic fly dressing materials. You name the material and there is an artificial substitute from tying thread, hair and even photographically produced replicas of plumage from rare or extinct birds.

The multitude of furs and feathers we use to tie flies have always come to us as a spin-off from other, larger industries, be it the millinery trade or production of food. Sadly, many natural materials are things of the past due to the destruction of wood-lands, wetlands and remote wilderness areas by agriculture and pollution.

THE SATURDAY EVENING POST

An Illustra... Weekly
Founded A? D? r ... . Franklin

MAY 25, 1918   5c. THE COPY

PAINTED BY NEYSA McMEIN

GASSED—By MAJOR S. J. M. AULD

Above: Feathers for flies and fine hats hastened the demise of many exotic birds.

How the fly developed

From those ancient Macedonian flies to our own creations, the truth is that things have changed very little in the design and construction of our flies, despite the passing of seventeen centuries.

There are no specific methods given for dressing the flies of the ancients, but, as those old flies were tied in the fingers and without sophisticated tools, it is fairly easy to work out a modern tying method.

THE DONNE FLY

First, the Donne Fly. Take a hook, without an eye of course, and run a waxed silk the full length of the shank to the bend. Then take a piece of white horsehair, either in a single strand or several twisted together, and lay it forward along the underside of the shank from the bend.

Bind this down with the silk and at the front of the hook, tie in the wing material which is a section of speckled partridge wing (my interpretation of the fly) laid so that the tips protrude forwards over the hook.

Bind the butts of the feather fibres down towards the bend. Trim off the waste and then dub the waxed silk with dun wool or fur. Wind the dubbed silk forwards to the point where the wing is tied in and then take a needle and split the wing fibres into two equal bunches.

Carefully wind several figure of eight turns around the bunches to keep them apart and then push them back over the body into a natural position. Take several turns of silk against the roots to lock them in position and finish the fly. There we have the Donne Fly, a very historic fly.

Tail   None.
Body   Dun wool or fur.
Rib   None.
Wing   Speckled partridge wing.

1. Take a piece of white horse hair, single or twisted strands as required, and lay it forwards along the underside of the shank from the bend. Bind this in place with the silk and then, at the front of the hook, tie in the wing material, which is a selection of speckled partridge wing (my interpretation of the pattern), laid so that the tips protrude forwards of the hook. Bind the butts of the feather fibres down the shank towards the bend.

2. Trim the waste off and then dub the silk with dun wool or fur. Wind the dubbed silk forward to the point where the wing is tied in.

3. Take a needle and split the wing fibres into two equal sections. Carefully tie several figure of eight turns around the wings to separate them fully and then push them back over the body into a natural position.

4. Take several turns against the roots to lock them into position.

5. There we have it. A simple and historic fly.

PLAIN HACKLE FLY

Next comes Charles Cotton's Plain Hackle Fly. There are several dressings, but the essentials are the dark body with a red or black hackle wrapped around it from tail to head. It sometimes has a silver or gold rib along the body.

Interestingly, of all Cotton's flies, only the palmer patterns have wound hackles and any mention of hackle feathers in his other flies are as wings.

After arming the hook with white horse hair, a rough body was formed from dubbed-on black spaniel fur or black ostrich herl and then a red cock hackle was wound along the whole length of the body. Then, as Cotton says "view the proportion and if all be neat and to your liking, fasten."

This then would be the way that Walton or Cotton would have dressed the flies that have remained successful today and which spawned their many offspring.

It is fascinating to realise that when you take a good look at our modern flies just how little things have changed.

THE GOLD RIBBED HARE'S EAR

The Gold Ribbed Hare's Ear, probably the oldest fly still being used, was thought by many to have first been tied without wings. It was and still is, a great catcher of trout, especially when fished in the surface film.

We would call it an emerger and it is fair to say that the GRHE was the pioneer of this important fly dressing style.

During the purist Halfordian era around the turn of the century, the wet fly was frowned upon as being unsporting and so some of the most successful wet flies were given wings and sometimes hackles.

The Gold Ribbed Hare's Ear was far too good a fly to escape the respectability treatment and it has retained its fish taking powers in spite of the alteration. Whether the wings actually improved its performance is debatable.

Silk Yellow or primrose.
Tail Three or four strands of hare's fur (as body).
Body Dark fur from root of hare's ear, picked out at the front to suggest the legs.
Rib Fine, flat gold tinsel.
Wing Pale starling wing.

1. *Start at the eye and take 15 turns of silk down the shank and then two open turns forward again to the middle of this silk 'bed'. From a matched pair of starling primary feathers, one from each wing, select two equally wide slips of feather and make a pair of wings. Offer these up to the hook so that they will be equal in length to the body (shank) and tie them in with a Pinch and Loop. Bind the butts down towards the bend and trim in two or three steps as you go to taper the body.*

2. *When almost at the bend, catch in a bunch of longish straight hairs from the hare's ear, to act as a tail. Take a length of size 1 fine, flat gold tinsel and tie it in under the hook, at the bend.*

3. *Pick some dubbing fur from the base of the hare's ear. Spin it fairly sparsely onto the silk and form the body almost up to the wing roots.*

4. *Follow this with the gold tinsel, wound in three or four open turns, also tying it in just short of the wings.*

5. *Make a loop in the thread by taking it around your finger and then back to the hook taking the thread over the shank, making one full turn round the shank and then one full turn round the double thread to close the loop before taking the thread forward to the front of the thorax. Work some dubbing into the loop.*

6. *Spin it into a "rope" and then form a thorax by winding it both behind and in front of the wings, setting them upright as you do so.*

7. *Tie off the loop and whip finish.*

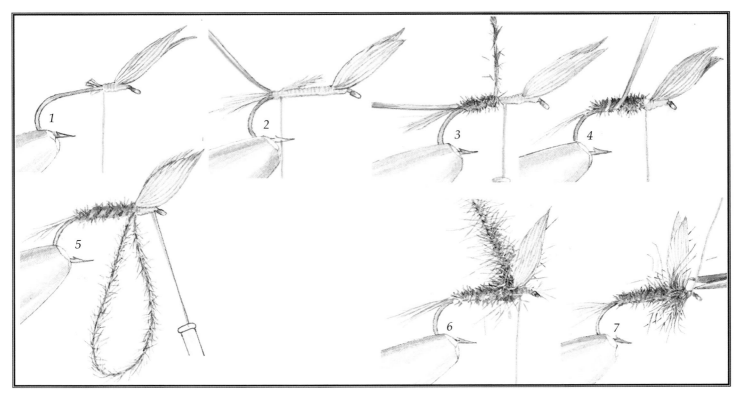

The construction of GRHE ensures that it sits low in the surface film and is an excellent general imitation of an emerging insect.

Far more up to date is the style of dry fly dressing developed by American fly fishers Doug Swisher and Carl Richards. These free-thinkers set out to design the perfect dry fly using photographic techniques.

They took pictures of natural insects from every angle, including from underwater, to get a better idea of how the trout sees a floating fly. They decided that the normal wound hackle used on most dry flies was probably the most inefficient way of suggesting legs although it was a very good way of keeping a fly afloat.

Their dry fly has no hackle at all and it is balanced only by the slight thorax area and "set" of the tail. The dressing method is important but the colouration is infinitely variable to suit the insect being copied.

Compare the No Hackle fly of the 70's with the Donne Fly of 1490 and a non-fly dresser could be excused for thinking that absolutely nothing had changed except for the addition of a tail. This is not quite so of course. Truth is that the development of the fly has simply come full circle.

THE NO HACKLE DUN

Tail   *Cock hackle fibres.*
Body   *Either fur, such as rabbit, or modern synthetic dry fly dubbing.*
Wing   *Duck shoulder feathers, paired.*

1. From the eye, wind the silk to the bend and then, with a very small amount of dubbing, form a tiny hard ball. Take the silk forward to the mid shank area and catch in a small bunch of six to eight cock hackle fibres. Separate these into two bunches on either side of the hook and bind them back along the shank to the dubbing ball. By tying them tight up against the dubbing ball they are forced apart by as much as 90° forming outriggers to balance the fly on the water.

2. Spin additional dubbing on to the silk and complete the body to about two thirds along the shank.

3. Take two or three turns forward and then tie in the pair of wings, with the tips towards the rear of the fly. Lift them up almost vertical and set in place by taking several turns of silk close up behind them.

4. Spin on more body dubbing and form a thorax both behind and in front of the wings. Whip finish. Note the splayed wing position on the finished fly.

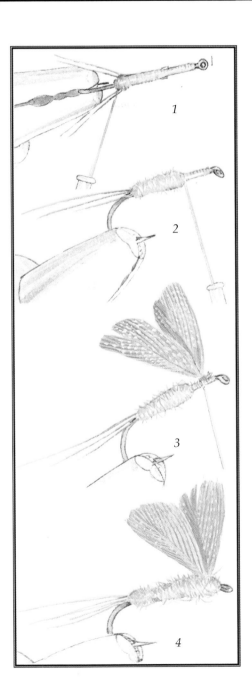

THE WINGED WET FLY

Somewhere between Charles Cotton's addition to The Compleat Angler in 1676 and the 1830's, the winged wet fly came onto the scene.

The Butcher was a front runner and was meant to imitate a small fish or a swimming beetle with its silvery air bubble. More modern thinking reveals that many insects produce sub-cutaneous gases just before rising to the surface and that these gasses shine a bright silver. This is particularly true of the midge or chironomid tribe. A black one has a dash of red at the tail end and I would say that this may be part of the Butcher's success story.

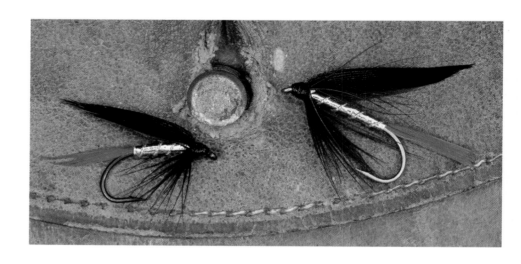

THE SILVER BUTCHER

Tail	**Red Ibis.**
Body	**Flat silver tinsel. I prefer the modern lurex types.**
Rib	**Oval silver tinsel.**
Hackle	**Black hen or soft cock.**
Wing	**Blue feather from a mallard's wing. Crow secondary feather is a good alternative.**

1. *Starting at the eye, take eight turns of thread. Tie in the hackle by the butt and pointing forward. Take the silk towards the tail in close touching turns, binding down the hackle stem as you go. Trim off the stem just short of the bend.*

2. *With the last turn of silk, tie in the red ibis tail, making sure that the butt ends reach forward to the point where the hackle is tied in.*

3. *At the bend, catch in a strand of fine oval tinsel, making sure that the butt end also reaches the hackle. Wind the silk back to the hackle.*

4. *Catch in the flat silver tinsel immediately under the hackle and bind down the butt with three forward turns.*

5. *Carefully form the body in close touching turns down the shank and then back again finishing off just in front of, and underneath,* the hackle. *Bind down the tinsel with three turns of silk back to the hackle. Wind the rib forward in four or five open, even turns and catch in under the hackle with three or four forward turns of silk.*

6. *With your hackle pliers, wind the hackle two or three turns forward to the silk and tie in with two turns. Remove the waste.*

7. *Pushing downwards from the top with your left finger and thumb, sweep the hackle fibres down and back, then bind the silk back onto the roots a little to hold them in position.*

8. *Prepare two wing slips and tie them in above the front of the hackle.*

9. *Tie down the butts and trim off the waste fibres. Form the head and whip finish to complete the fly.*

THE PALMERS

The Zulu is probably the best known of all the simple palmer style flies. It has been around for a long time and probably evolved from the ancient Plain Hackle, the only real difference being the addition of a red tail and silver rib.

It is a good stillwater fly, fished either wet or dry, usually on the top dropper as a bob fly where it is dribbled across the ripple to imitate a hatching insect. The Kate McClaren, Red Palmer, Soldier Palmer and so on, are merely variations on the theme and are dressed in much the same way.

THE BLUE ZULU

Tail   *Red wool, feather fibre or floss silk.*

Body   *Black ostrich herl, wool, seal-fur or floss silk.*

Rib   *Silver tinsel – originally fine flat, but I have a personal preference for oval.*

Hackles
    Body – Black cock wound sparsely down the body.
    Front – Bright blue cock.

1. Starting at the eye, take ten touching turns of silk towards the bend and tie in the black hackle. Make just a couple of turns. Next, catch in the blue hackle and bind down both hackle stems with another ten or so turns. Trim off both stems, leaving one just longer than the other.

2. Take a piece of red wool or preferred tail material and catch it in with one turn of the silk, making sure that the butt end reaches forward to the point where the blue hackle is tied in. This will help to avoid unsightly bumps when the body is formed. Now, take the silk back to the bend in touching turns, keeping the red wool on top of the shank all the way.

3. Tie the ribbing tinsel in underneath the hook with one forward turn of silk, again leaving a butt that reaches forward to the blue hackle.

4. Tie in the body herl with the next forward turn of silk and bind down all material butts forward to the blue hackle in order to avoid any bumps. Take the silk forward to one turn in front of the black hackle. Wind the ostrich body herl forward to the tying silk and tie it off with two full turns.

5. Attach the hackle pliers to the black hackle, take one full turn in front of the blue hackle at the front of the body and then wind it towards the bend in open turns catching the tip in with one turn of the rib. Maintaining tension on the rib, wind it forward through the hackle in even,

open turns and tie it off with two more forward turns of silk. If you trap a few fibres of hackle in the process, these can be picked out again later with the aid of a dubbing needle. Take the silk forward to within three turns of the eye.

6. Take the tip of the blue hackle in your hackle pliers and wind it forward in touching turns.

7. Tie it off and form a small, neat head.

Dressed in this fashion, the Blue Zulu is an ideal bob fly, being nice and bushy but, if a sparser form is required, it is easy to adjust the amount of front hackle used or to strip away one side of the body hackle.

THE SPIDERS

Traditionally known as North Country Spiders in Britain and, more recently as Soft Hackles in America, these thinly-dressed flies are the fore-runners of the modern nymph.

Spiders are old by any time scale and have been faithfully recorded for well over a century.

Dressed in the main with lightly dubbed silk bodies and soft hackle feathers taken from a great variety of birds, Spider style flies offer a very close suggestion of the nymphs, emergers and drowned insects.

Many of the feathers are unobtainable now as they came from protected species and as a result, some of the old Spiders have become part of fly fishing history.

However, we can still dress most of them. One classic is the Little Dark Watchet, an imitation of the Iron Blue dun and a firm favourite on cold springtime days.

THE DARK WATCHET

Hackle	Jackdaw's neck or wing covert from a coot.
Body	Orange and purple silk twisted and dubbed with down from water rat or mole.
Head	Orange silk.

1. From the eye, make five turns of orange silk and catch in the hackle by the tip. Wind the silk towards the bend, catching in a length of purple silk as you go. Stop opposite the hook point.
2. Work a very sparse amount of dubbing onto the orange silk and twist the two silks together into a "rope".
3. Form the body forward as far as the hackle and then separate the two silks. Catch in the purple silk with the orange and trim off the purple.
4. Wind the hackle forward for two turns and tie it off.
5. Form a small, neat head with the orange silk and whip finish. Trim away the waste orange silk.

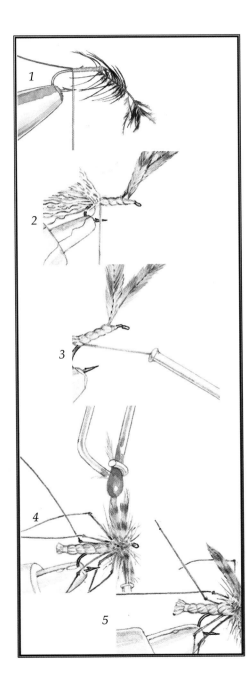

The chalk stream influence

Inspired by the spartanly clad Spiders, Skues developed his famous nymphs which probably did more to shape modern fly fishing than anything else, particularly on England's southern chalkstreams where the dry fly tradition had stifled innovation for so long.

Skues made himself most unpopular for arguing strongly in favour of the return of wet flies to these hallowed streams where they had been in common use when he was a child. Despite being branded a heretic by the establishment, he fought a strong case.

His persistence paid off and the modern fly fisher owes him a debt of gratitude.

His patterns are simplicity itself and show the beginnings of the modern nymph with a tapered body or distinct thorax hump. The Medium Olive Nymph is a classic example.

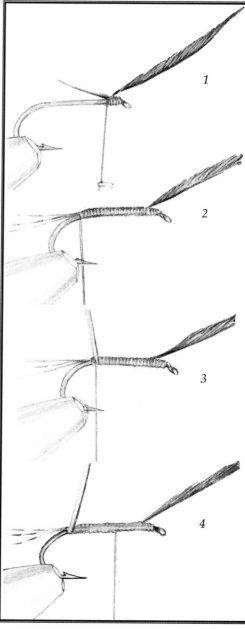

THE MEDIUM OLIVE NYMPH

Hook	*Size 14-16.*
Silk	*Purple or grey-brown waxed with dark wax.*
Abdomen	*Brown peacock quill.*
Rib	*Silver wire (optional).*
Thorax	*Dark hare's ear.*
Hackle	*Dark blue dun.*
Whisks	*Short, dark guinea fowl.*

1. From the eye, take five turns of silk and catch in the hackle.

2. Wind the silk in touching turns to the bend, catching in the three tail fibres as you go. They should be tied in short – about the length of the hook gape only. If using a rib, tie it in now, under the hook at the bend.

3. Take a peacock herl, strip off the flue and tie it in under the shank.

4. Take the silk two thirds the way up the shank then wind the quill in touching turns up the hook. Follow this with the rib if used.

5. Dub the silk with hare's ear fur and form the thorax forward to the hackle.

6. Wind two turns of hackle forward and tie off.

7. Whip finish to complete the simple but highly effective nymph.

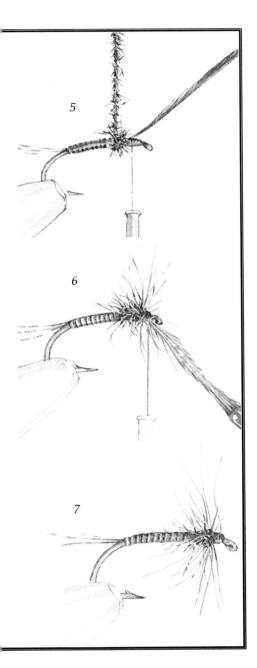

5

6

7

The dry fly story

The quill for the classic Medium Olive Nymph is taken from ordinary peacock herl but, if we take a herl from the peacock eye itself and strip that, we get a quill with dark and light sides.

When wound as a body, this quill forms contrasting bands along the body which imitates the natural abdomen and forms a basis of many of Halford's patterns.

Halford was a dry fly purist and would not countenance the use of wet fly, nymph or even anything slightly damp. He was responsible for the Gold Ribbed Hare's Ear being given wings to make it "respectable" enough to be used on the chalk streams.

The Blue Quill is the classic Halfordian style of dry fly, and as successful today as ever it was. It was based on the much older English Westcountry fly, the Blue Upright. A hackled version of this fly is more typical of the Westcountry style.

The Blue Quill

Silk   *Yellow.*
Wings   *Light starling.*
Body   *Stripped peacock quill, undyed.*
Hackle   *Pale blue dun.*
Tail   *As hackle.*

1. Take 14 turns of silk from the eye and then back, in open turns to the middle of the silk bed. Tie in a pair of matched wing slips with the tips facing forward in the advanced position.

2. Take three turns towards the rear and there tie in the prepared hackle by the stem.

3. Continue winding down the shank towards the bend, trimming off the wing butts and hackle stem in two or three steps, to aid the formation of a slightly tapered body.

As you near the bend, catch in the tail whisks with the last turn rear-wards.

4. Catch in the prepared quill. Take the silk forwards to the hackle and carefully wind the quill body to the hackle.

5. Tie this off immediately in front of the hackle and wind the silk forwards to the front of the wing. Lift the wings upright and then take several turns of silk tight in front of the wings to stand them upright. Take the silk forward to within four turns of the eye.

6. Wind the hackle forward and catch it in by the tip.

7. Tie it off at the eye and whip finish.

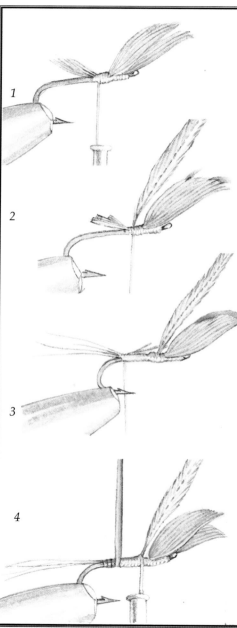

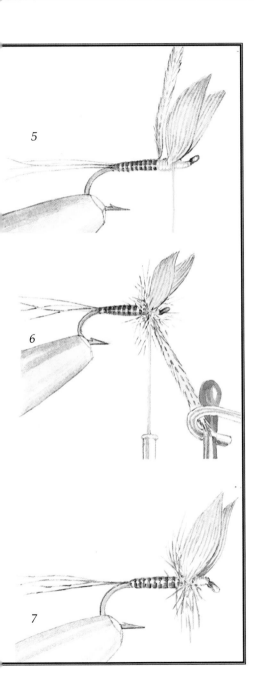

5

6

7

Around the turn of the century, William Lunn was working on a range of imitative patterns on the River Test where he was keeper on the famous Houghton Club at Stockbridge.

In 1916, he revealed a range of flies developed after years of study of the natural insects and their behaviour on his beloved stream. All were fashioned from easily found materials and worked well. One, the Lunn's Particular is one of the best known traditional dry fly patterns still in use today. Originally dressed to imitate the olive spinner, it has since earned a reputation as a good general fly during a hatch of olives. While usually dressed with wings tied flat in the spent style, the fly can also be fished with them cocked upright during the earlier part of the hatch and before the spinners start to fall onto the water.

THE LUNN'S PARTICULAR

Hackle Medium Rhode Island.

Wings Two medium blue dun hackle tips.

Tail Four fibres of Rhode Island hackle.

Body Undyed, stripped hackle stem from a Rhode Island cockerel.

Silk Pearsall's No. 13 Crimson. Sadly hard to find these days but either shade 12 or 14 will do.

The wings for this fly need special preparation. It is important that the fibres on the lower part of the stem are trimmed off with scissors rather than stripped off which will weaken the fine stems.

1. From the eye, take 14 turns of silk and then a couple of open turns towards the eye, lay down a base of silk on which to tie the wings. Tie in the paired wings on edge and in the advanced position with the tips facing forward.

2. Make just two turns behind the wings and tie in the hackle. Take the silk to the bend and there, catch in the tail fibres.

3. Strip the hackle stem body and tie it in by the tip. Take the silk forward to one turn in front of the hackle. Wind the body forward showing just a single turn of silk at the bend.

4. Lift the wings to the vertical and wind two or three turns in front of them.

5. Spread the wings to the horizontal. To set the wings in place, take a turn between the wings to the rear, round the hook one full turn and then forward again between the wings and then one full turn round the shank. Wind the hackle for two turns behind the wings and then two turns in front of them.

6. Whip finish for the completed fly.

Another famed river keeper was responsible for advancing nymph fishing an important step further down the development trail. Frank Sawyer, keeper on the Officers Water on the Upper Avon in Wiltshire had, like Lunn, spent hours on end watching the natural fly life and more importantly, the behaviour of the trout to the different flies.

From what he saw over many seasons, Frank developed a small range of simple but lethal flies which he used as much to remove unwanted grayling from the water as they were for trout.

Probably the most famed of his flies is the Pheasant Tail Nymph, a fly whose fame has spread all around the fly fishing world. Simplicity itself to tie, this fly imitates almost any form of river-born fly nymph as well as many stillwater flies.

Normally fished on a floating line, the nymph is weighted to sink and is then cast upstream and allowed to drift back down past a bottom-feeding trout. Sometimes it is brought to life by lifting the rod tip, a simple technique known as the Induced Take for which he is also famous.

Frank only passed away a few years ago and I am proud to say that I knew him quite well, albeit for only a short time.

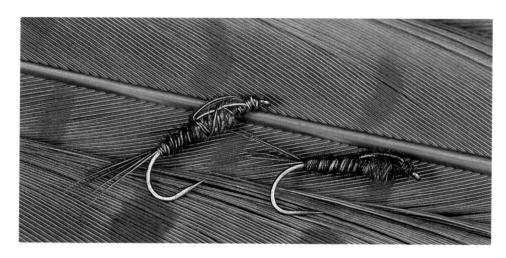

THE SAWYER'S PHEASANT TAIL NYMPH

Hook   *Size 10, 12, 14, or 16.*
Body   *Cock pheasant centre tail.*
Silk   *None. The fly is dressed and weighted at the same time with fine copper wire.*

1. Take about a foot of wire and starting just behind the eye, wind it tightly onto the shank for about a third of the hook. Build up several layers to form a thorax hump.

2. Wind the wire to the bend and there catch in five or six pheasant centre tail fibres with two turns of wire. The tips should form a short tail equal to the width of the hook gape.

3. Grip the pheasant tail and the wire together and then wind them all forward to the front of the hook and in front of the thorax.

4. With the fibres on top of the hook, wind the wire to the back of the thorax in two open turns. Fold the fibres back and catch them in with two turns of the wire.

5. Wind the wire forward again in two open turns and fold the fibres forward.

6. Catch in with two turns of the wire, form two half hitches at the eye. Trim off the feather fibres and twitch off the waste copper wire.

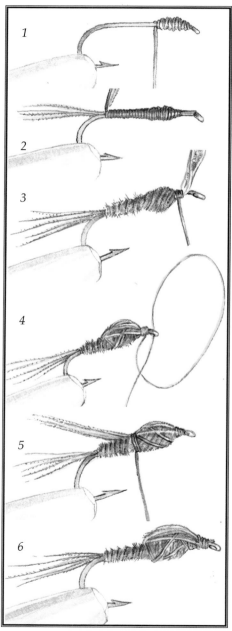

The Invicta is credited to English fly dresser James Ogden of Cheltenham. I say that because, apart from the winging feather, it is identical to the Great Hackle or Palmer Fly revealed by Charles Cotton in his list of flies for May written over 400 years ago.

Be this as it may, Ogden was responsible for much fly tying development. Although best known these days as a lake fishing pattern, especially when the caddis or sedges are hatching, it is likely that it was originally an evening fly for Brown Trout and migratory Sea Trout. It is one that beginner fly dressers find difficult to tie as it has a palmered hackle wound over a seal fur body fronted by a jay hackle which should be wound.

THE INVICTA

Hook	*Size 10 – 14.*
Tail	*Golden Pheasant topping.*
Body	*Yellow seal fur.*
Rib	*Gold oval.*
Hackle	*Red game cock palmered down body.*
Throat	*Red game cock and blue jay wound in front.*
Wing	*Hen pheasant centre tail.*

The most difficult part of this fly is in the preparation of the jay hackle since it is necessary to peel the fibres from the main feather, leaving them attached to a sliver of quill only. Unless prepared in this way, it would be almost impossible to wind the hackle as the stem is so thick. The hackle is tied in either by the tip or butt depending on which wing it has been taken from so that the blue is facing forwards. Some people overcome this difficulty by tying in a simple beard hackle made from a few fibres pulled off a jay feather, but the wound hackle looks so much better.

1. From the eye, take ten turns of thread and tie in the hackle.

2. Take the thread to the bend and tie in the tail and oval gold rib.

3. Dub on the seal-fur and form the body forward to the hackle. Wind the hackle one full turn at the front and then wind in open turns to the bend.

4. *Catch in the hackle with the rib and wind this forward in even, open turns.*

5. *Catch in the jay hackle and wind two turns forward.*

6. *Pull the hackle fibres down and back and form an even bed of thread in front, just angled enough to hold the hackle in place.*

7. *Prepare and tie in a pair of wings.*

8. *Whip finish to complete the fly.*

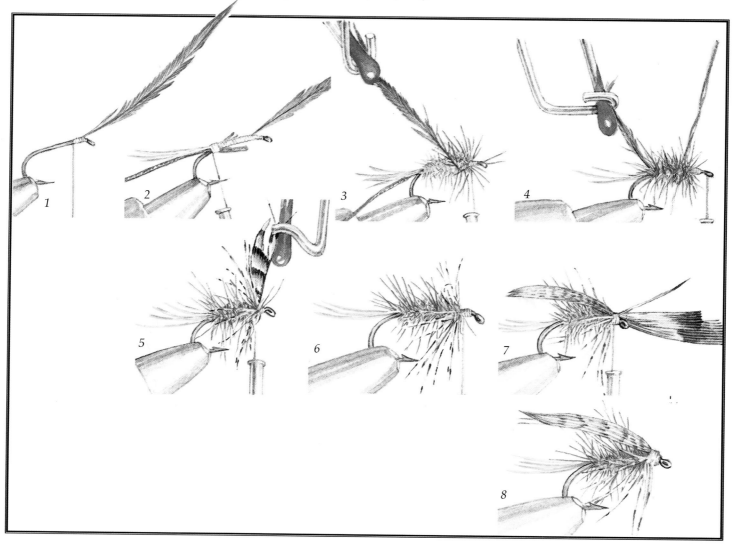

The stillwater scene

*The building and stocking of drinking water
reservoirs in Britain sparked off the rapid
development of imitative flies.*

Perhaps the best known of these forward-thinking fly dressers was Doctor Bell who fished the Blagdon reservoir near Bristol. Those early flies were the basis of much of what we tie and use on all still waters today.

I have a sneaking feeling that the Invicta may have played a part in the development of one of my favourite patterns, the Amber Nymph, which is now a first fly choice when trout are busy snacking on sedges. He designed two versions, one the Large Amber Nymph, the other the Small Amber Nymph, the only difference between the two being the colour of the thorax. I used the original version for years until I became more observant and less impulsive. Since most caddis pupae have marked segmentation on their bodies, I gave the fly a rib to satisfy my need for "exact" imitation.

I also dressed a dark claret version inspired by that other great traditional favourite, the Mallard and Claret. The dressing of the Amber Nymph is very simple with the added bonus of being one of the most killing flies we can offer.

Next page: Becalmed on an English stillwater.

THE AMBER NYMPH

Hook	Size 10 for the large and size 12 for the small. I tie them down to size 16.
Body	Amber seal-fur or floss tied thick.
Wing	Grey-brown feather strip tied over the body only.
Thorax	Brown seal-fur or floss over the front third of the hook.
Legs	Pale honey hen sloping back from under the head.
Rib	My own addition is gold or copper wire tied in at tail and wound on top of wingcase as far as the thorax. Some of the modern pearl materials also make excellent ribs.

1. Take the thread from the eye to the bend or even a little way round it to give a curve to the body. Catch in about 12 pheasant tail fibres by their tips.

2. Dub on the amber seal-fur and form the body over the rear two thirds of the shank.

3. Pull the pheasant tail fibres over the back and tie them in. Dub on some brown seal-fur and form the thorax.

4. Take a small bunch of hen hackle fibres and tie them in under the front of the thorax so that the tips just reach as far as the point of the hook.

5. Trim off the butts of the hackle fibres and form a neat head. A slightly shaggy finish is desirable as it traps air bubbles in the fur.

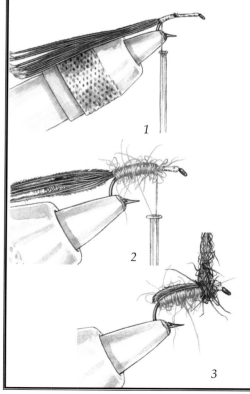

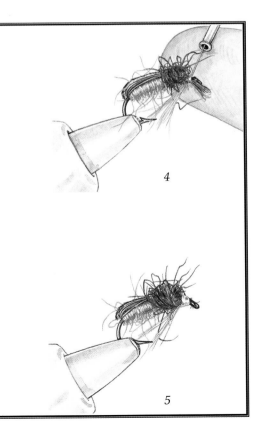

4

5

THE BUZZER STORY

The chironomids or midges are of tremendous importance to all stillwater fly fishers. Dr Bell, of Blagdon reservoir fame, started the buzzer ball rolling in Britain with a simple, yet highly effective imitation. Because the insect is so high on a trout's menu, free-thinking fly dressers the fly fishing world over have taken the original idea much further, but most flies are still based on the essential trigger points of a slim body, plump thorax and the white, frond-like gills found on the rising pupa.

Fishing the imitations causes problems for many fly fishers, simply because they are fished far too quickly. The most effective retrieve rate ranges between dead stop or just a shade faster.

ALL IN THE THORAX

As flies have become more imitative, the swelled thorax area has become an important feature of our imitations.

Nymphs tied with an under layer of copper wire or fine lead for deep fishing on a floating line, or dressed un-weighted for fishing on a sinker, probably account for the largest proportion of trout caught anywhere that they swim.

It is impossible to say who started the prominent thorax theme going. In England it was probably that world-famed master of the nymph style, Frank Sawyer who introduced the Pheasant Tail Nymph.

Whoever started it, the idea was soon carried over to a whole host of nymphs and bugs. The shrimps and corixae were among the first to receive the shellback treatment. The other special style of weighted nymph that has influenced modern fishing styles world-wide is the Stick Fly. Useful on waters both running and still, these flies come into their own when there are no obvious signs of fish feeding either near or on the surface. As trout spend most of their time grubbing around on the bottom, it makes sense to use a weighted fly and on a strange water, it should be a first choice.

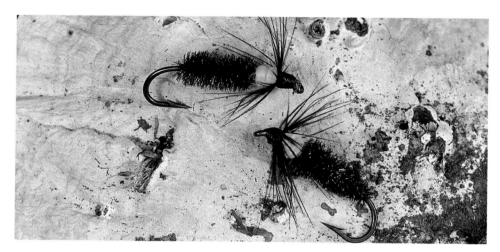

THE STICK FLY

Body **Peacock herl. Hare or rabbit fur are good alternatives.**

Thorax **A collar of green, yellow or white wool.**

Hackle **Sparse soft black cock hackle or partridge hackle.**

Head **Made larger than usual and well varnished to be really glossy.**

1. Take ten turns from the eye and catch in the hackle. Take the thread onto the bend and wind an under-body of lead wire almost as far as the hackle. Bind the thread forward and then back over the lead to anchor it down.

2. At the bend, tie in the peacock herl and then wind this forward with the thread. By winding them together they will twist into a strong rope.

3. Tie in the thorax wool and wind it forward to the hackle. Tie in with two turns in front of the hackle.

4. Wind the hackle for two turns forward and tie it in.

5. Form a larger than average head and give it several coats of varnish to make it shine.

Dry Fly Developments

Returning to the dry fly theme, it is well worth looking at one or two developments which have occurred away from the powerful English influence prevalent for most of the last century and a half.

From the times of the Treatise onwards, the humble duck, both wild and domestic, has provided winging feathers for trout flies.

Look at these historic dressings and you will see mention of the barred flank and breast feathers of the mallard and similar ducks, and there is no doubt that these flies were the basis for a most famous style of fly developed in America. Known today as the Catskill style, these effective dry flies originated in the Catskill Mountains and their names are inextricably synonymous with Theodore Gordon.

A feature of this type of fly is the Lemon Wood Duck winging material. I am told that it is chosen for its availability, strength and durability.

The tying method I use follows that of the Dette family who have tied them since the late 1920's.

I met both Walt and Winnie Dette while researching this book and saw the Catskill style at first hand when I visited their home on the outskirts of Roscoe.

The Quill Gordon illustrates this style well and just one look at the fly confirms its historic origins.

Normally dressed on larger hooks than those generally used by English dry fly dressers, the special feature of the style is the distance back from the eye that the head is actually finished. It is not uncommon for bare shank to be exposed behind the hook eye, something I find very hard to make myself do.

THE QUILL GORDON

Hook   Size 10 – 14.

Thread White or pale yellow.

Tail   Originally Wood Duck but more recently dun hackle fibres.

Body   Stripped peacock eye quill.

Hackle Dun cock hackle. Usually two wound together.

Wing   Lemon Wood Duck in two bunches.

Properly dressed, this fly uses two whole feathers for the wings. There is a modern tendency to dress it with a small bunch of fibres torn from a feather since it is more economical, Wood Duck feathers being rather hard to acquire these days.

1. Bunches of fibres torn from a single feather.

2. The original method. Make a bed of silk taking care to leave a small amount of bare hook at the eye. Take the two wings and pair them back to back.

3. Stroke them from butt to tip several times to pull the fibres up really close and then tie them on in the advanced manner. Lift them up to the vertical and form a figure of eight around the roots.

4. Take the thread to the bend, trimming off the butts to form a gradual taper and then catch in the tail fibres.

5. Catch in the prepared quill, take the thread forward almost to the wings and then wind the quill body.

6. Tie in two dun cock hackles and take the thread forward. Wind the hackles one at a time. This is quite easy as long as the second hackle is kept taut as it is being wound through the first one.

7. Whip finish the completed fly.

8. The same fly shown head on illustrates the natural curve of the wing gained by using this method.

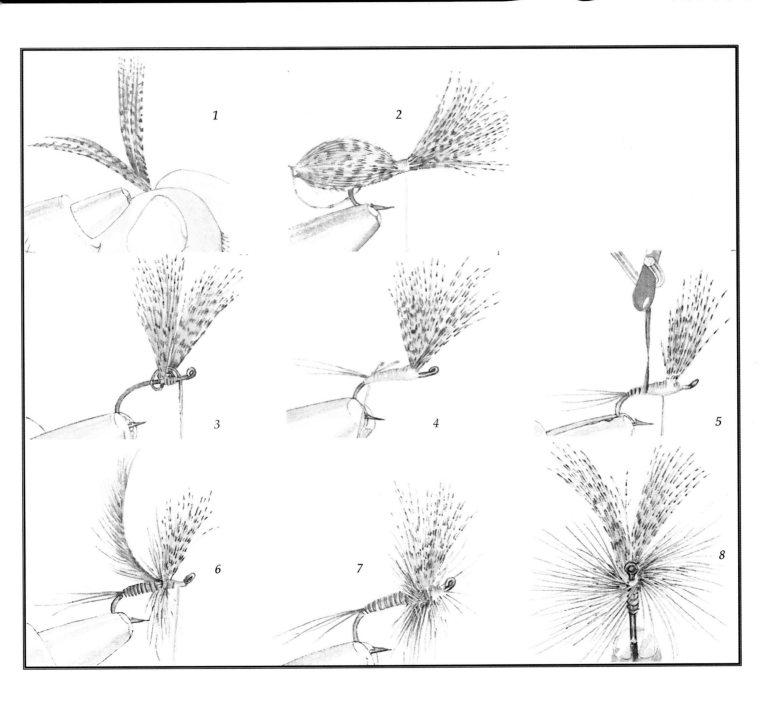

1

2

3

4

5

6

7

8

Another duck feather, this time the frond-like and oil-laden plume found around the preen gland, has revolutionised dry fly fishing. Used in Europe for many years, Cul de Canard feathers can be used as hackles, as wings or even wing cases on emerger patterns.

The most interesting use in my opinion is the method made popular by Marc Petijean who employs the delicate feather in a unique way. His flies do not have conventional hackles and sit low in the water to give them extra fish appeal.

One of his specials has a bunch of Cul de Canard plumes sloping back over a body of wound Cul de Canard like a sedge fly. Another, more complex pattern, has a body and thorax of wound Cul de Canard with a wing of the same feather split into two clumps by some floss silk, pulled over the thorax and then tied down at the head.

THE CUL DE CANARD

Hook Size 12-20 or even smaller.
Tail Cock hackle fibres.
Body Wound Cul de Canard feather.
Thorax Wound Cul de Canard feather.
Wing Cul de Canard feather fibres stripped off and bunched. These are split into two clumps with a length of floss silk tied in at the rear of the thorax and then pulled forward over the completed fly and tied in at the head.

The colours for the flies are based on the natural flies being imitated. Natural, dark olive, and pale yellow being particularly popular.

1. From the eye, prepare a bed of thread in the usual way. Onto this, tie a pair of Cul de Canard feathers or a bunch of fibres stripped off the plume.

2. Take the thread to the bend and tie in the tail.

3. Take a large Cul de Canard plume and tie it in at the bend. Tie it approximately at its centre with two turns and then pull it by the stem until it is bound only by the tip. This whole feather is then twisted and wound up the shank to just behind the wing to form the body.

4. Tie in a couple of strands of floss silk to match the colour of the fly. Tie in a large Cul de Canard plume by the tip as for the body and take the thread forward.

5. Twist the Cul de Canard plume and form the

thorax both behind and in front of the wings.

6. Separate the wing plumes into two and pull the floss silk forward between them to keep them split. Tie down and trim off.

7. Form a small neat head and whip finish to finish the fly.

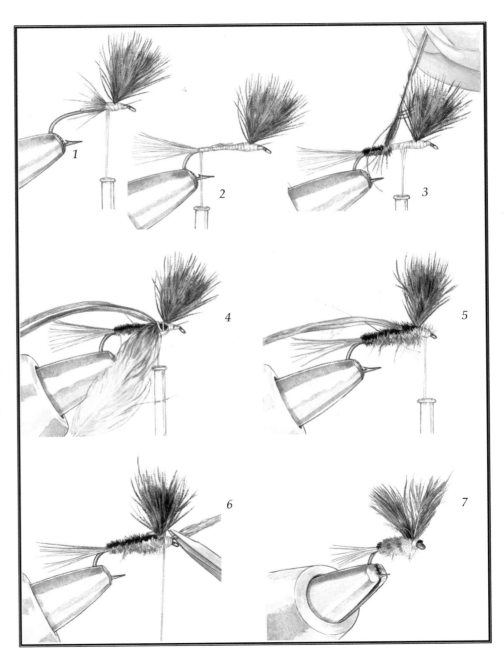

Deer hair is used for winging as well as for bodies. One of the most famous hair wing dry flies known throughout the world is the Grey Wulff. Devised by American fly fisher Lee Wulff, it was probably the first true hair-wing dry fly.

While fishing the Ausable River in New York State on Labor Day in 1930, Lee set out to imitate a large greyish mayfly after failing with the traditional English style of mayflies. He turned to hair for both wings and tail and created a superb fly that radically changed dry fly thinking in the process.

Lee Wulff scorned a fly vice and dressed the flies with his fingers, a knack he demonstrated into his 80's. He added the White Wulff and the Royal Wulff a little later before other fly dressers jumped on the hair wing bandwagon with their own variations on the theme.

THE GREY WULFF

Hook   *Size 8-16 (larger sizes are used for salmon).*
Tail   *Natural brown bucktail.*
Body   *Grey Angora rabbit.*
Hackles *Blue dun, at least two for good floatation.*
Wing   *Natural brown bucktail.*

1. From the eye form the usual thread base for the wing which is then tied on in the advance position. The wing is then separated into two bunches and then set upright with figure eight turns of thread.

2. Take five or six turns of thread from the wing towards the bend and then tie in one hackle with two turns followed by another hackle. These are tied in and trimmed whilst the thread is wound to the bend where the tail is tied in.

3. Dub the thread with fur and form a body forward to the front of the hackles.

4. Wind first one hackle forward and tie off and then the second which is wound through the first and then tied off at the front.

5-7. The finished fly seen at different angles to show the correct shape of the wings.

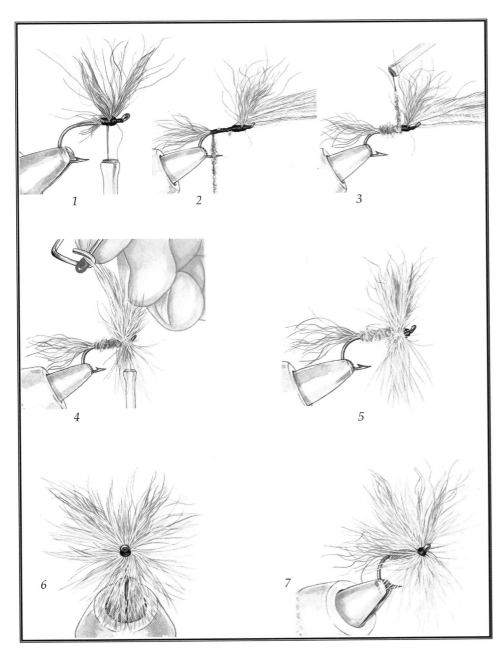

1
2
3
4
5
6
7

It seems that every fly dresser knows that deer hair flares and spins when tied onto a hook. Fewer realise that this varies from deer species to species and more importantly, from the head to the tail on each animal.

Deer hair can be categorised into three textures. Fine, which has almost no flair. Medium, which will flare out to about 45° and the coarse kind which springs out very readily. Knowing how each one behaves allows the fly dresser to pick and choose the right kind of hair for the fly in mind. Always remember that the finer the hair, the less buoyant it will be.

A modern dry fly that illustrates this well is the Elk Hair Caddis devised by American fly dresser Al Troth.

Various hair wings have been introduced over the years, this one sets the standard. I have seen them dressed in all sorts of sizes and colours and think it best to see the fly as a special style in its own right rather than as a particular fly. Some are dressed without the hackle so that the fly sits low down in the surface film while others sport bleached hair making them easier to see.

THE ELK HAIR CADDIS

This is one of my favourite versions of the most useful pattern.

Body	**Grey dubbing, natural fur or synthetic dry fly dubbing.**
Rib	**Light tying thread. Wire or hackle stem are good too.**
Hackle	**Dun cock hackle.**
Wing	**Natural brown elk.**
Head	**Butts of wing fibres clipped off to protrude over the eye.**

1. Take eight turns of thread from the eye and tie in the hackle. Take the thread to the bend.

2. Lightly dub the thread and wind it forward to the hackle. Take one turn in front and then dub back to the tail.

3. Wind the hackle for two full turns at the front and then palmer it down the body to the bend where it is caught in with the tying thread. This tying thread is spiralled up the body in even rib, tying in the hackle as it goes.

4. Remove the waste tip of hackle and either trim off some of the top fibres of the hackle or stroke them down onto the sides a little. That done, take a bunch of elk hair, the tips evened up in a stacker, and tie it in immediately in front of the body with three or four turns of thread.

5. Lift the butts up and back so that the head is formed in front. Trim off the butts leaving a short raised stub to imitate the head.

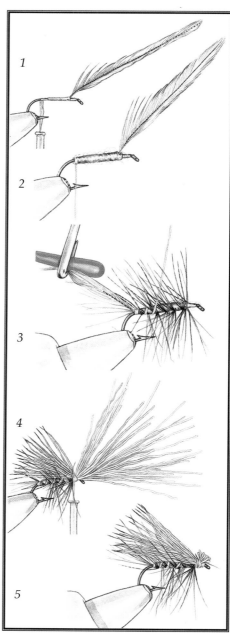

Enter the lure

Dry flies and small insect representations aside, nothing has caught the fly dressers' imagination more than the attempts to imitate little fry and baitfish.

While in England fly fishers were content to stay with their wet flies tied on lengthy tandem mounts, their fly fishing brothers in America and New Zealand employed far more radical and realistic thinking.

The streamer tribe of lures were among the first of their purpose-designed fish imitators with a body of tinsel, wool or coloured floss and very long feathers streaming out behind the hook. One which has been re-discovered by British stillwater anglers is the Black Ghost, a lure first tied in 1927 by Herbert L. Welch.

I frequently use the modern single-strand body floss in a bobbin holder and tie part of the fly with this instead of using normal tying thread.

THE BLACK GHOST

Hook	*Longshanks in a wide range of sizes.*
Tail	*Yellow hackle fibres.*
Body	*Black floss heavily dressed and tapered at each end.*
Rib	*Medium flat silver tinsel.*
Throat	*Yellow hackle fibres.*
Wing	*Four white hackles.*
Cheeks	*Jungle cock.*
Head	*Black.*

1. Catch in the floss about mid-shank and bind it first forward and then back again to the bend. Catch in the hackle fibres for the tail as well as the flat tinsel ribbing. Work the thread forward again and then back again, building a plump but tapering body.

2. At the eye, catch in the tying thread. Wind it to the front of the body and tie off the body floss. Wind the rib in even turns to the front of the body.

3. Tie in the throat hackle immediately below the front of the body.

4. Prepare four cock hackles for the wings, making sure that any slight curvature is matched on each side. Either strip or trim the fibres off the stem to the correct length and place two on each side so that the 'good' sides are facing out. The natural curve then keeps the wing closed when they are tied on.

5. Set one Jungle cock feather on each side of the wing. Build up a neat head and whip finish.

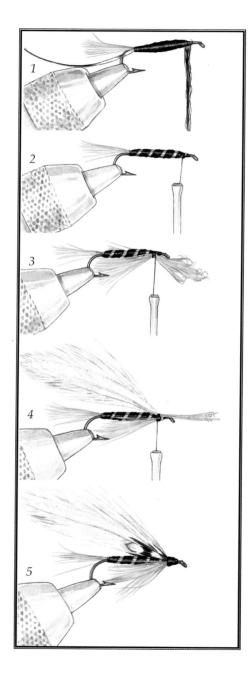

There is one particular bucktail with a style all of its own. Exported 30 years or so ago from America and Canada, the Muddler, devised by Don Gapen of Minnesota who tied the first ones to imitate a flathead minnow, is now a firm resident in the boxes of fly fishers the world over.

Performing well on both floating and sunken lines, the Muddler Minnow is certainly here to stay.

THE MUDDLER MINNOW

Hook Longshank. Size 2-12.

Tail *Natural speckled turkey wing. Tie it just longer than the hook gape.*

Body *Flat gold tinsel.*

Wing *Grey squirrel tail with a slip of speckled turkey wing either side. The hair should reach just past the tail and the feather as far as the tail tip.*

Head Black.

Shoulder – Natural deer hair spun on with the first spinning leaving tips that reach back to form a collar almost as long as the wing. The remainder is clipped to shape, but keep it flattish on top like the natural minnow.

1. Starting about half way down the hook, take the thread to the bend and tie in the tail and gold body tinsel. Take the thread back to the starting point and then form the body.

2. Take a bunch of grey squirrel tail fibres and tie these as a wing with the tips reaching to the end of the tail.

3. Take a turkey quill and work a slip of fibres until they stand out at right angles and are level at the tips. Fold this slip in half and tie it in to shroud the hair wing.

4. Take a bunch of deer body hair and offer it up to the fly with the tips reaching to the bend of the hook. Tie this in so that it spins around the hook to form a collar.

5. Repeat this spinning with further bunches of hair after trimming their tips. Pack the hair after each spinning. A useful tip when doing this is to make sure that the cut portion of the hair bunch is much shorter than the tips because it will be easier to avoid trimming off the fine tips needed for the collar at the completion of the fly.

6. Push all the hair well back and whip finish with a small neat head.

7. Trim the clipped deer hair to the desired shape leaving the collar intact. A razor blade is better than scissors for the trimming, but be careful.

8. The completed fly.

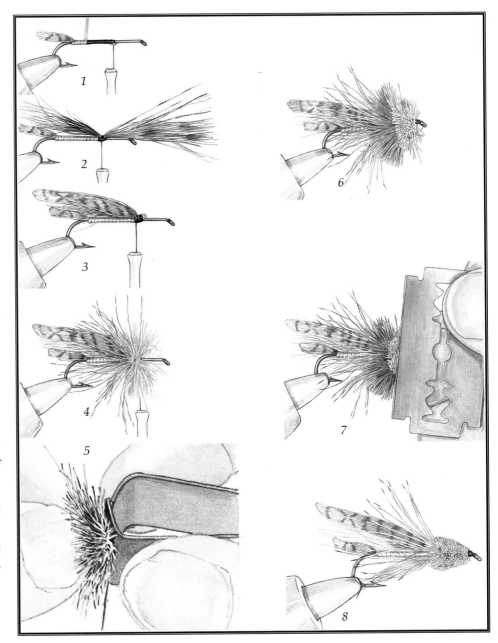

The Matuka style lure was taken an important stage further with fur strips being used instead of feathers to create a distinctive crest-like wing. The original was called the Rabbit. It took years before other fly fishers looking for an effective baitfish imitation caught onto the Rabbit idea but once they did, all sorts of variations hit the headlines even to the stage where they were re-named Zonkers. What is in a name – it is the idea that's important!

So well known had the style of lures become, that packets of rabbit skin, sliced sliver-thin were soon available, the skin itself being soft-tanned for maximum movement in the water. The Black Rabbit is typical of the multi-membered Rabbit or Zonker family.

THE BLACK RABBIT

Tail *Red wool.*
Body *Black chenille.*
Rib *Oval silver tinsel.*
Wing *Thin strip of rabbit fur on skin tied in with the ribbing in the same manner as for the Matuka.*
Head *Black varnish.*

1. From the eye, take the thread to the bend, catching in a length of red wool for the tail. Make sure that the waste end of the wool reaches well forward to where the body will finish. At the bend, catch in a strand of oval tinsel and the prepared chenille.

2. Wind the chenille forward to make the body and then tie in the rabbit strip by the tip.

3. Pull the rabbit strip tightly over the body and catch it in with the rib Matuka style. Leave a short length sticking out beyond the bend. Wind the rib forward, trapping the rabbit strip with each turn.

4. Tie off the rib at the front.

5. Form a head and stroke the fur back – strip a few times to make it lay well. Whip Finish.

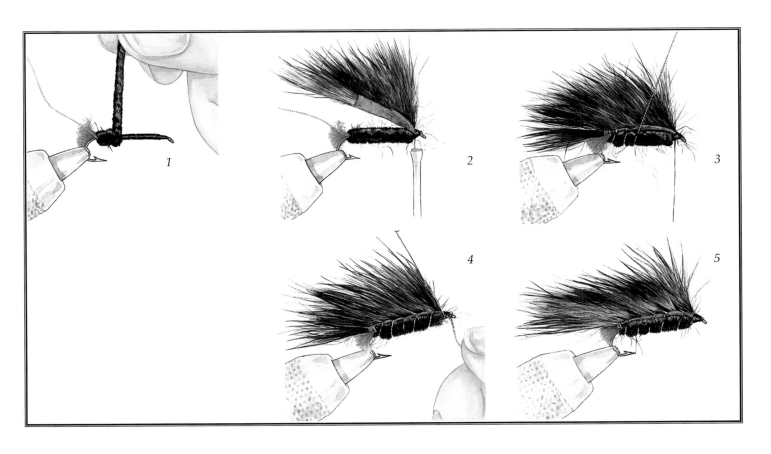

1

2

3

4

5

Flies around the world

As an English fly fisher and dresser, I tie patterns to suit my own local conditions and I guess the same applies to others like me around the fly fishing world.

Above: An Italian Spider style wet fly.
Below: The Pallarette. Bottom: Mave.

Almost without realising it, what we know as established local patterns have been influenced by the techniques and ideas trickling in from wherever trout are tempted with fur and feather.

It is a fact though, that fly dressers wherever they fish have come up with parallel ways of thinking, simply because their creations have been designed to suit the same kind of water conditions.

Striking examples are the simple flies from Seisa Valley in Northern Italy. They are remarkably like the English North Country patterns complete with the slightly unusual set of the hackle which is cocked forwards and the silk tied off behind it. These flies, both in England and in Italy, were designed to fish wet or just in the surface film in fast-flowing streams.

Simple they may be to look at and tie, but they are well worth trying wherever the water flows quickly.

A typical dressing, and how simple can you get, is just a purple silk body and a black hen hackle tied on hooks ranging from sizes 10-18.

More modern Italian flies are similar and differ from their ancestors only in that the bodies are fashioned from fluorescent flosses or sport brightly coloured heads.

Similar flies are found in New Zealand and in South Africa as well as in Spain. However, some Spanish patterns involve tying methods all of their own, two in particular being something very special.

The Pallarette is a most distinctive fly with a varnished, straw-yellow silk body tied into a plump carrot shape with the dark blue dun hackle tied on top and then pulled back. The Coq de Leon hackles used by the Spaniards are things to drool over.

Another Spanish pattern which also uses the same feathers is a spider style fly tied in a very different way to take full advantage of the very long and glossy hackles, which cannot be wound in the usual way as they are so springy.

The body is dressed, ribbed and then a bunch of fibres is pulled from the spade hackle feather and carefully slipped over the fly from the front to form a sparse, but glittering halo around the fly.

A fly called Mave has a primrose head, purple silk body ribbed with the same primrose silk and the hackle is a mottled golden spade hackle feather known locally as Pardo flor de escoba.

Getting nearer home, there is a fly known to fly fishers world-wide and that is the Coch y Bonddu. This is an imitation of the

Opposite: Such objects are the makings of a fly dressers dream.

Bracken Beetle, the body is tied plumpish and is very beetle-like.

I have witnessed a fall of these little beetles just once in Hampshire, a long way from its home in wild Wales. Like many Welsh flies, this beetle imitation has a thickish body formed from peacock herl tipped at the tail end with just a couple of turns of flat gold tinsel which is also used to rib the body. The hackle feather is much used on Welsh patterns and is a darkish natural red with a black centre and tips.

Look at the flies from any country and you will find beetle imitations. The Australians have their Tri-Tree Beetle which they fish either wet or dry.

It is a fly well worth having, even when beetles are not about in any numbers. The dressing is quite simple with a black ostrich herl body, a black cock hackle and a shell-back which reaches the whole length of the body formed from a strip of brown feather.

Beetle patterns using deer hair have been around for some time and are getting more popular by the season. An outstanding example of the American deer hair beetle are those tied by the famed Dette family.

Simplicity itself to dress, they float like corks. One which we should all have ready has a peacock herl body and a black dyed deer hair back with the legs being formed by trimming some of the deer hair strands.

While deer hair is buoyant, more modern beetles use closed-cell foam instead. It goes without saying that a similar design, but using non-buoyant materials, is ideal for imitating all manner of aquatic beetles and a change from black to a white or pale body

is quite good enough to fool trout guzzling on corixa.

Adding a tiny silver tag at the tail adds to the illusion of a silvery air bubble, as will a dubbing which traps air.

Having gone underwater, perhaps we should stay there a while longer and talk about imitations of nymphs and little fish.

There are many ways of imitating these tiny fry. There is one we should all try and that is the Thunder Creek style perfected by America's Keith Fulsher. Surprisingly, little has been seen of this superb little fly. One well worth tying is the Silver Shiner which incorporates many of the features found in baitfish imitations the world over.

The Silver Shiner is best dressed on a longshank hook. The tying silk is bright red and the body flat silver ribbed with oval

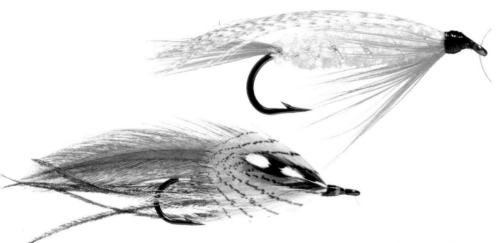

Left to right: Coch-y-Bonddu, Australian Tri-Tree Beetle, Dette Beetle, Silver Shiner, Corixa, Grey Ghost and Missionary Lure.

silver thread. The back is formed from brown bucktail and the under-belly from white bucktail. It has a large distinctive eye formed by painting on yellow with a quite large black pupil.

An eye-catching feature of the Shiner is that the wing and belly are tied in so that the hair tips face over the eye and are then pulled back and tied down after the rest of the fly has been tied. For added strength, the hair butts are varnished before the hair is drawn back as is the whole head and red gill whippings to give a hard gloss finish.

This style of working with bucktail is a logical progression from the work achieved by Maine fly dresser Carrie Stevens, who used the method on her salt water flies. The wings are much longer and stiffer than found on most streamers and are glued together in units before being tied in.

The American streamer flies differ a lot depending on where they are fished. The Western flies have their wings cocked up high to counteract the roaring rivers while others, designed with far more gentle flows in mind, have their wings tied flat against the top of the hook. These slimmer flies are intended to imitate injured or tiny fish scattered by a marauding trout.

English fly fishers thought along the same lines when they adapted the original Missionary lure to make it flutter down through the water from side-to-side to imitate an injured fry sinking to the bottom.

New Zealand fly dressers follow much the same theme with their own lake flies. These very different looking flies were originally dressed with plumes from the Pukeko bird, but as these feathers are no longer available, mallard flank feathers dyed either black or blue are used instead.

The Pukeko and Red is typical of the tribe and is dressed with a red wool tail, red chenille body river with silver and three blue Pukeko feathers tied flat over the body. There are two other special fly styles that are important in the development of the trout fly internationally and which can loosely be described as lures rather than imitators. They have both been well known in South Africa for decades although there may be a New Zealand connection in their history. The first one is a double-hackled fly called the Red Setter.

THE RED SETTER

Hook   Longshank.
Body   Hot-orange chenille.
Hackles Red game.
Tail   Red squirrel tail.

1. Start the thread at the eye and take it down to the bend and there tie in a bunch of red squirrel tail fibres and the hot-orange body chenille. Take the thread down to the mid-point of the shank.

2. Wind the chenille almost to the mid-point and tie it off. Take the thread forward three turns and tie in a red game cock hackle.

3. Make three forward turns of the hackle and tie it off. Now pull the hackle back at an angle and tie back onto it so that it is swept back sharply. Tie in more hot-orange body chenille and start the forward half of the body.

4. Tie off the chenille at the front of the fly and then tie in and wind the front red game hackle.

5. The front hackle is swept well back and then the head is formed to complete the fly.

There are several similar flies, of which probably the best known, is the Fuzzy Wuzzy with its red body and black hackles and tail.

The Walker's Killer is a South African favourite and is one of a number of patterns that incorporate sides rather than wings. This pattern has been in and out of fashion during the last 30 or 40 years.

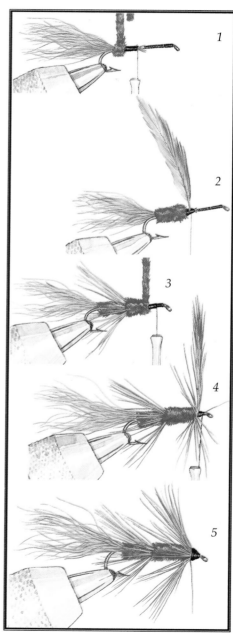

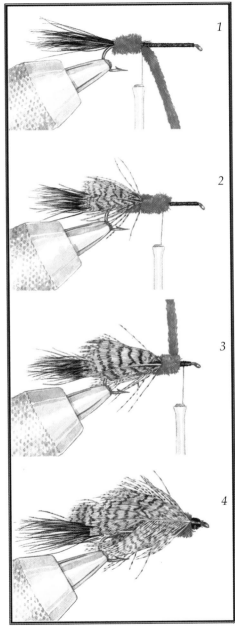

THE WALKER'S KILLER

Hook *Longshank.*
Body *Red chenille.*
Flanks *Three pairs of partridge flank feathers.*

1. *From the eye, take the thread down the shank to the bend and tie in a tuft of black squirrel tail fibre followed by the red chenille. Take the thread forward one third the length of the body and wind the chenille.*

2. *Take a pair of partridge flank feathers, preferably showing a central stripe and tie one flat on each side of the fly. Tie in more red chenille and form another one third section of the body.*

3. *Tie on a second matched pair of partridge flank feathers and form the final third of the body with red chenille.*

4. *At the head, tie in yet another pair of partridge flank feathers. Complete the fly with a whip finish.*

Mrs. Simpson and the Mallard and Yellow lures are dressed in a similar way with the pairs of feathers tapering towards the tail.

The larvae of the caddis or sedge flies have always been high on the fly dressers' list and of the none-case makers, the white or cream Hydropsyche and the greeny-olive Rhyacophila, which look rather like caterpillars, have long occupied fly dresser's minds.

There is a fly dressing from France which resounds in the name of Plantereuse, which I particularly like.

Dressed on size 12 and 14 hooks, the body, after being weighted with copper or lead wire, is covered with golden yellow wool or a synthetic dubbing and then ribbed with yellow silk. The hackle is a single turn of brown partridge and the head made quite large.

Dressings on this grubby theme are found the fly fishing world over and it is

not easy to say who tied them first. A recent and very useful variation from Yugoslavia includes a gold bead at the head which apart from adding glitter, makes the fly sink really well. Silver and copper beads are now also being used.

Whether it is the gold or silver or just the depth at which these flies fish that makes them quite so attractive I cannot say, but they are most certainly very useful things to have in the fly box.

On some streams, the Stone Fly family figures high on the trout's menu for the day. Some of the flies tied to imitate the adults are ancient but there is no doubt that the best of the nymph imitating patterns hail from America.

The one most widely used just has to be the Montana Nymph. The original, formed

by wrapping black chenille over a heavily leaded base, has black hackle fibres or a couple of black goose biots for the tail and a yellow chenille thorax which sprouts a black hackle along its length. The wing-case is simply another length of black chenille pulled over the yellow thorax.

This old stager has spawned more than its fair share of variants and it is not uncommon to see them dressed with a green or even a bright red thorax.

A similar fly called Ted's Stonefly has a tail of brown goose biots, a brown chenille body and wing-case and a similar coloured hackle wound over an orange chenille thorax while the Bitch Creek Nymph has tails fashioned from white rubber strands, a black chenille body with a length of orange chenille tied underneath and held

Left to right: Plantereuse (top), Gold Head (bottom), Ted's Stonefly (top), Bitch Creek Nymph (bottom), Montana Nymph (top) and Wriggle Damsel (top).

in place by tying thread rib and a black thorax over-wound with a brown hackle.

The bigger the nymphs go, the more difficult it is to give them a semblance of movement.

One way is to add flowing marabou tails. This is not a modern idea by any means since marabou winged fry imitations were used way back in 1910.

The Wriggle Nymph really brings things up to date. Made famous by American fly dressers Carl Richards and Doug Swisher, every conceivable kind of nymph, is treated to this way of tying.

The Damsel Nymph is typical, being dressed in two parts with a long shank hook used for the body and a shorter one for the thorax and head.

THE WRIGGLE DAMSEL

***Rear hook** – A straight-eyed 2 or 3 X long shank hook.*
***Tails** – Three very small hackle tips tied in a horizontal plane.*
***Body** – Olive to insect green floss silk, herl or fine dubbing dressed fairly slim.*
***Rib** – This is optional and you can use fine wire or monofilament.*
***Front hook** – Weighted if needed.*
***Thorax** – Hare's fur or a similar dubbing to match rear body colour.*
***Wing-case** – Folded raffine or a C de C plume for the emerger version. Use feather fibre for the normal nymph.*
***Eyes** – Burnt nylon or pearl eyes for the emerger. I use bead chain for the deep fishing version.*

***Hackle** – Partridge or a grizzled hackle dyed to match the body colour.*

Not a difficult fly to dress, the tails and body are tied on a longshank hook and then the hook bend is broken off to leave the dressed shank. Put the shorter front hook in the vice and secure down a length of five pound nylon to point over the bend. Thread on the dressed body and then bind the free end of the nylon forwards on the front hook.

Adjust the loop so that the eye of the rear hook almost touches the front hook and put on the rest of the materials. Easier done than said, it is quite easy to tie midge nymphs down to size 18 although at that size there is no need to use a long shank for the rear hook.

There have been so many attempts to imitate insects in the act of hatching that we have coined the term emerger to cover the dressing style. One of the best has to be Dutch fly dresser Hans van Klinken's Klinkhammer Special which pools all the best ideas into a single fly.

Hans dresses the fly on size 12-22 sedge or grub hooks with a light tan dry fly dubbing body taken well around the hook bend. Peacock herl forms the thorax, the wing is a tuft of white poly yarn and the hackle a shiny chestnut colour.

THE PARACHUTE GREY DUSTER

Thread Brown.
Body Wild rabbit fur containing both under fur and guard hair.
Hackle Badger.

The following method is the simplest way of completing this type of fly.

1. From the eye, take the thread to the centre of the shank and there tie in the prepared hackle with four or five turns. then make a loop in the stem and catch this in again at the same point, only with just two turns of thread. Take the thread to the bend.

2. Dub the thread and wind forward to the eye and whip finish.

3. Take three or four turns of the hackle around the loop stem making sure that each turn is kept below the previous one. Keep the hackle pliers level with or below the shank as you wind.

4. Maintain tension on the hackle as the tip is passed through the looped stem.

5. Pull gently on the end of the stem so that the loop gradually closes trapping the hackle. Trim off excess hackle.

6. Trim off the waste stem and place a drop of varnish in the centre of the hackle to complete the fly.

Below: Klinkhammer Special.

The Parachute hackle can also be tied around the root of a wing using a polypropylene wing and is a style much favoured for modern emerger patterns as the fly sits low in the water.

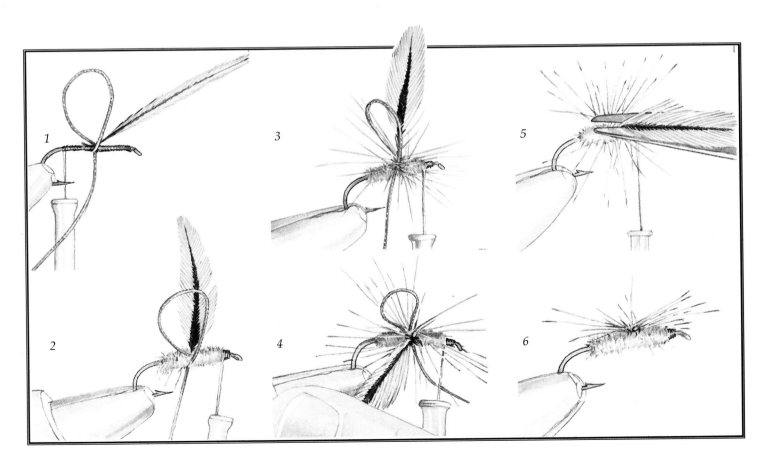

THE PARACHUTE HACKLE

1. Form a thread base on the middle of the shank and tie in the hair or poly yarn. Set this wing upright and take three or four turns around the wing root only.

2. Take the thread to the bend of the hook and form the tail and abdomen forwards again to the wing root.

3. Tie in the hackle flat, immediately behind the wing and take the thread just forward of the wing. Trim off waste hackle stem.

4. Wind hackle round the root of the wing, keeping each turn lower than the previous one, three turns usually being sufficient, and then drop the hackle trip downwards to the vertical. Bring it just forward of the hanging thread, but not completely under the hook and then lift it up again to the horizontal. This will trap the hackle tip between the thread and the far side of the hook shank. Bring the thread round the shank two full turns to tie the hackle tip in place, taking care not to tie down the hackle fibres.

5. Form the front half of the body and whip finish. Whilst doing all this, it is necessary to hold the wing and front hackle fibres up and back gently and it is this stage that makes the second half of the tying technique a little tricky for beginners.

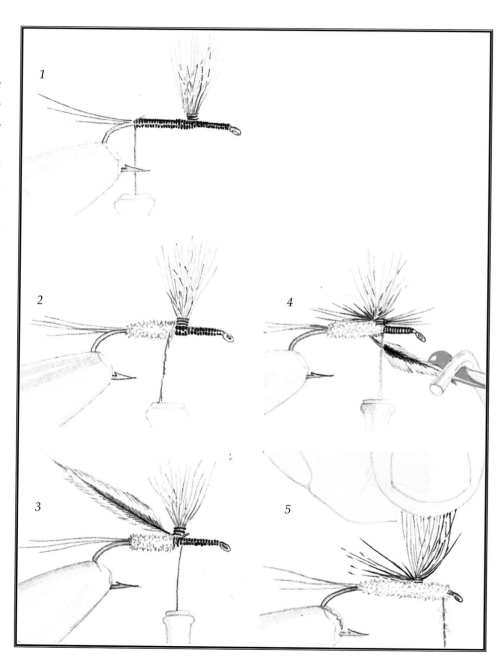

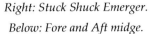
Right: Stuck Shuck Emerger.
Below: Fore and Aft midge.

Most new patterns are destined to enjoy brief quick-silver fame, their ultimate fate being to follow thousands of others into obscurity.

Failure has never daunted the fly dresser and the search for the ever-elusive ultimate fly will continue.

One of my own flies, originally designed to imitate the crippled and highly vulnerable mayfly dun looks promising.

In much smaller sizes, it has proved a real winner on the America's Delaware River, a far-cry indeed from its home on the English Derbyshire Wye.

To dress the Stuck Shuck Emerger, you need a size 10 Tiemco 400T or Partridge Taff Price Swimming Nymph Hook.

The tail is fashioned from brown-dyed grizzled marabou feather tips. The rear third of the body is made by twisting the rest of the tail materials into a rope and then winding it thinly around the hook. The contrasting front portion is formed from a pale creamy olive dubbing which is also used to form a raised thorax. The hackle is olive dyed grizzle and the wing, originally a mixture of olive and brown elk, can also be made from natural Cul de Canard feathers. Both are tied 'short' to avoid masking the hook point which is way out of line on this specially-shaped hook.

The hackle on this fly, and on most of my patterns, is wound palmer fashion over the thorax area and then clipped into a wide, splayed 'V' underneath.

Flies with hackles tied fore and aft are popular in Britain and Europe but deserve a wider audience. Whilst not a particularly specialist fly dressing technique, it is worth a mention since the style creates a really buoyant fly as well as a passable imitation of those flies unlucky enough to have fallen onto the water during the mating act. Certainly there are times when trout pay special attention to this double helping.

For this reason alone, it is well worth carrying imitations of the sedge tribe and Black Gnats dressed on long shanked flies with hackles at front and rear.

Tying techniques and step-by-step instructions

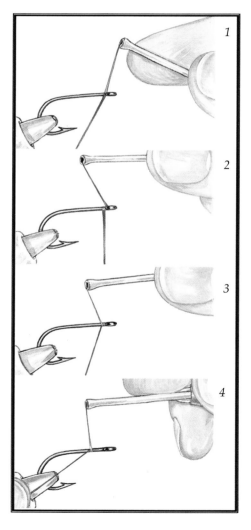

STARTING THE THREAD

1. Holding the bobbin holder in the right hand and the end of the tying thread in the left so that the thread is taut, offer it up at the eye of hook so that the bobbin is above and left hand below the shank.

2. As the thread rests up against the shank, the bobbin is taken away over the shank and round the hook for the first turn.

3. When this first turn is completed the thread is angled slightly towards the rear of the hook so that the second turn traps the thread against the shank in the form of a whipping.

4. Each successive turn should touch and travel towards the rear of the hook. A useful aid to ensure close touching turn is to keep the spare end of the thread taut and pulled out at an angle to the hook shank so that each subsequent turn of thread slides forward to lie tight against the one in front.

Tip – The working thread should be kept short, say an inch from bobbin tube to hook, as it is so much easier to wind a short one around the hook rather than the usual three or four inches many beginners struggle with. When using a bobbin, grip the collar where the arms join the tube between forefinger and thumb, while the other fingers maintain a little pressure on the actual thread spool in the palm.

THE WHIP FINISH – Two handed

To practice, use a large hook and heavy, well-waxed thread you can both see and feel.

1. Extend the thread to about six inches in length and hold it taut below the hook and inclining towards your waist with the left hand. Place the first and second fingers of the right hand onto the thread.

2. Rotate the right hand clockwise by 180° and then slightly lift the hand to form a triangular loop. Properly done, the fingers are inside this loop and thread from the bobbin to the right hand is horizontal and resting on top of the section of thread coming down from the hook.

3. Lift the right hand up in front of the hook, slightly opening the fingers as you do so and the bobbin thread will be trapped under the hook by the other leg of the loop. The apex of the loop is then pushed away and down by rolling the right hand.

4. Transfer the thread to the finger and thumb of the left hand and complete the first turn almost to the top, where the thread is once again transferred to the right hand.

5. The thread can be taken on over the hook into the second turn, which is a repeat of the first.

6. Make at least three, but preferably five, turns

and then take up the tension of the loop on a dubbing needle with the bobbin lifted to allow the thread to lay almost alongside the body.

7. Keep the tension in the loop with the needle as you pull on the thread bobbin. Always pull in line with the hook not at right angles to it.

8. As the loop pulls tight, slide the needle out for the complete whip.

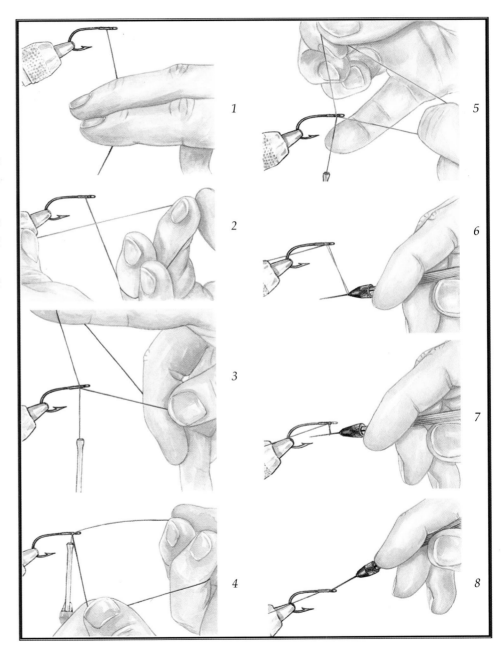

THE WHIP FINISH – Using a tool

Until the advent of the rotating versions of the whip finish tool, I was not a fan of such gadgets and still insist on my able-bodied students learning a hand-whip finish. The technique learned, treat yourself to one of the Materelli type.

1. Grip the tool at the base of the rear hook so that the hook cannot rotate. Catch the thread on the front hook.

2. Loop the thread round the double hook at the rear and take it forward again, taut.

3. Twist the tool slightly anti-clockwise, so that the handle is horizontal and the front hook vertically below the head of the fly. Transfer the grip onto the handle so that the tool can rotate freely. It will automatically revolve and form the triangle seen in the hand version.

4 – 5 Wind the tool over the hook and down the other side and it will revolve within its handle, forming the whip in the process. Repeat four or five times.

6. When complete, lift the hook to the vertical, when it will slide within the loop and:

7. Pull the lower 'double' hook out of the loop. Once the loop is on the single hook only, pull the bobbin thread until the loop closes, slipping the hook out at the last moment.

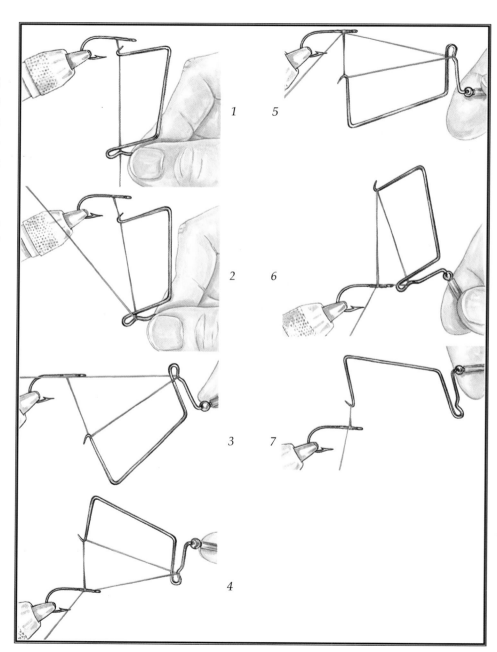

1

2

3

4

5

6

7

Preparing a Wing Slip from a Quill

1. Take a quill feather such as a mallard primary and with a needle, separate the required amount of fibres as one slip.

2. Stroke the slip from butt to tip, pulling it downwards slightly.

3. Grip the slip firmly between the first and second fingers of the left hand and pull it away from the stem. This pull should be at right angles to the stem rather than a gradual peeling motion.

4. The prepared slip should look like this, with a sliver of stem quill still attached. Wing slips cut from a quill tend to disintegrate.

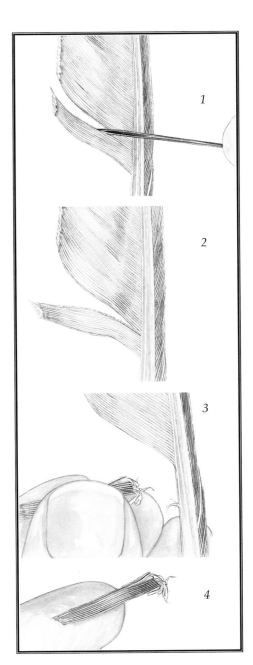

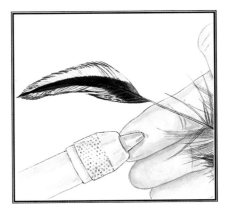

Preparing a Hackle Prior to Tying in.

A cock hackle should be prepared so that the side which will lay on the hook when wound has a few extra fibres stripped off. This helps to solve the twisting problem some tiers experience when they are winding hackle feathers.

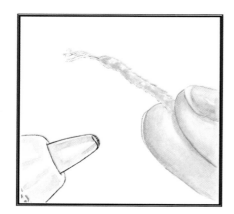

PREPARING CHENILLE

A close look at rayon chenille shows that the fibres are swept back in one direction, so it is important that the fingers stroke 'with the grain' as it is being wound.

THE PINCH AND LOOP

This technique has several names, depending on geography and is used to tie in various materials as well as for actually winging flies.

1. Take the prepared wing slips and offer them up to the hook so that the bottom edge is resting on the hook shank. The thread is taken up between the thumb and the shank, to the vertical.

2. Pinch tight and then bring the thread down on the far side between finger and hook shank, leaving a slack loop at the top.

3 & 4. Maintaining the tension with the left finger and thumb pull the loop downwards until the butts lift.

5. Repeat at least twice and only then release your grip and inspect the result.

This technique requires a degree of feel, so practice is essential to judge the correct degree of grip. Too much and the thread will not pull through, too little and the wings are likely to distort out of shape and line.

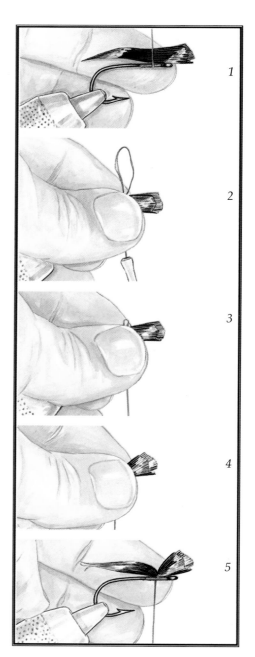

Fly dressing tools

It is quite possible to dress flies using no more than a sharp blade or a pair of scissors, but things are made much easier if you use the many tools designed specifically for the job.

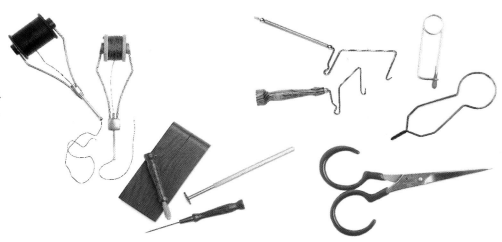

ESSENTIAL TOOLS

BOBBIN HOLDERS

While it is possible to tie flies without a bobbin holder, life at the vice is much easier with one as it holds the store of thread under tension leaving your fingers free for other tasks. I prefer a bobbin holder with a built-in ceramic tube as it prevents the thread chaffing and snapping at the critical moment.

DUBBING NEEDLES

These are an essential part of a fly dresser's tool kit and are used to pick up little bits of feather from the bench and to tease out the fur on the fly body or to separate wing slips from a main feather. You can also use one to apply varnish to the fly head although I prefer a fine brush.

HACKLE PLIERS

These are simple clips used to grasp the hackle making it easy to wind it around the hook. My own test for pliers, is to grip a hair on my arm and to see if I can pull it out. Reject any that fail this task as pliers that suddenly release their grip at a tricky moment are a real pain.

SCISSORS

Good scissors are essential and it is false economy to buy cheap ones. Look for fine points, not on the back and front as much as on the edges, as it is these that dictate how close you can trim away the waste materials after each step in the dressing process.

I usually grind and polish the back and front to the tips to a really fine taper, and try not to use my finest ones for cutting coarse ribbing materials or any heavy duty work.

THE VICE

Vices have been around for a century and more, starting with a very simple miniature vice operated with a wing nut. Modern vices are much more sophisticated with adjustable head angles, interchangeable jaws which rotate around a full 360 degrees and even motor drives. I prefer a lever-operated vice with rotating jaws and an adjustable head angle.

Above: Left to right: Bobbin holders, dubbing needles and a dubbing block, hackle pliers, whip finish tools and scissors.

OTHER TOOLS

DUBBING BLOCK

This is a simple wooden block with a pin at one end. A loop is hooked over the pin and one arm of the thread loop laid in a groove and the other held in a slot. The dubbing is laid on top of the silk in the groove, adjusted for density and then the other loop is removed from the slot and laid on top of the dubbing.

A dubbing twister is then hooked into the lower part of the loop and the fur-loaded threads twisted into a rope ready for securing to the hook.

DUBBING BRUSH

A velcro covered tool used to give a fly body a shaggy look. If you want a less straggly fly, then use a picker which is a very fine needle covered with tiny barbs.

DUBBING RAKE

Some dressers prefer a dubbing tool with a serrated edge which looks like a mini-garden rake.

DUBBING SPINNERS OR TWISTERS

The spun dubbing loop style is nothing new at all and relies on the use of a small, but heavy, spinning top. Attach the spring wire hooks into a long loop filled with fur strands and then give the bobbin a twirl. With a little practice, the result is a fur-covered thread looking much like a hairy pipe cleaner.

DUBBING WAX

This has been around for the past 200 years and is used to waterproof the tying thread, to stop the hook from going rusty and to help fur fibres stick to the thread. A great help when using coarse fibres, it can be a real nuisance with much finer furs like mole or muskrat underfurs which can be almost impossible to handle on a sticky waxed thread.

HAIR STACKER

This two-part tube is used to even up the tips of a bunch of hairs used for fly wings and those for dry flies in particular.

PROFILE PLATE

A light coloured disc fixed onto the vice to provide a neutral background while the fly is being tied.

WASTE BAG

A simple attachment for the vice to collect all those bits that fall onto the floor. Called the divorce saver by those who spin a lot of deer hair!

TOOL CAROUSELS

A multi-holed disc holding all the little tools onto the vice stem.

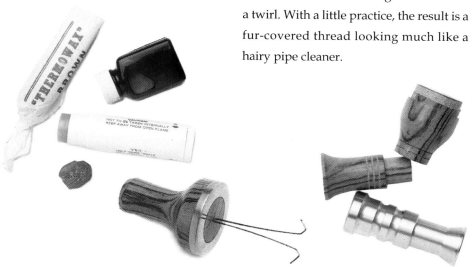

Above: Dubbing twister, varnish, waxes and hair stacker. Opposite: Fly dressing materials from around the globe.

Fly tying tips

The expert fly dresser can flicker fur and feather into a fly from what looks like an almighty jumble, but for lesser mortals, preparing the materials before the fly is started is as important as manual dexterity and fly tying know-how.

First, let us look at the all-important hackle feathers.

WAYS WITH HACKLES

Decide which side of the feather will face forwards and then remove all the soft fluff from the bottom of the little quill so that the side which lays on the hook as the hackle is wound, is slightly shorter.

Prepared in this way, the first turn of the hackle is made using the bare quill stem and you will find that it will not twist out of line.

I always tie normal hackles in by the bare stem except when using doubled cock hackles on exhibition wet flies. Then they go in by their tips.

When working with soft hackles such as grouse or partridge, tie them in by the tips after the fibres have been stroked to stand at right angles to the central quill. You will only use a couple of turns at the most.

Hen hackles can be treated as cock hackles and can be tied in by the stem, or like the soft hackles, by the tip.

WINGING TIPS

THE PAIRED SLIP WAY

Paired wings are fashioned from strongly fibred quills such as those found on duck and starling wings. The required width of slip is separated from the rest of the fibres on the feather by inserting the dubbing needle close to the stem and then sliding it up between the fibres.

Once separated, the slip is stroked from butt to tip while gently easing it outwards at right angles to the central quill.

The slip is then gripped firmly and carefully pulled off the stem. The two slips are paired, either with the tips curving together for a wet fly, or with tips apart if you are tying up a dry fly.

If the fly recipe calls for a rolled feather wing, then a wider, single slip is selected, removed from the quill and then folded or rolled into a single wing.

While primary wing feathers are normally used for flies with upright wings, some secondary quills such as those from hen pheasants are used as well, especially when tying flies with rolled wings.

Above: Top to bottom – French partridge hackle, English partridge hackle feather. Opposite: Furs of every colour and texture.

WHOLE FEATHER WINGS

Careful preparation is the key when tying in the fragile feathers used on flies calling for fan or hackle tip wings. Care must be taken to ensure that the feathers twin each other for size, shape and colour.

If centre feathers are used, take two side-by-side but, if side or flank feathers are called for, then make sure that they are plucked from exactly the same place on opposite sides of the bird skin.

If you use packeted feathers, you will have to do a lot of sorting, but the extra effort produces the perfectly balanced fly you are striving for.

When preparing these delicate feathers, trim and not strip off the unwanted flue or fluff with scissors. This way, the central stem is not weakened and the little stubs left on the feather make it much easier to tie in securely.

HAIR WINGS

Hair wings on both wet and dry flies can be neatly tied if you take care when trimming the hair from the tail or skin. As with feather slip wings, the little bunch of hair should be pulled out at right angles before it is cut away.

Even up the hair tips in a stacker if you are tying wings on a dry fly but leave them "rough" if you looking for a nice taper to a wet fly or streamer wing.

To keep any hair wing secure, add a tiny drop of head cement to the trimmed roots before they are finally tied in. Some hard hairs, especially squirrel, will not compress even under quite hard tension and have a tendency to pull out no matter how well you tie them in.

Wings formed from synthetics such as antron or polypropylene can be tied in as a single bunch or by folding back or upright, a longer length fixed by its middle on top of the hook.

Some synthetics are used in simple sheet form and are usually folded or trimmed to a wing shape. It is not that good for upright wings as they tend to flutter and spin in the air, although this is less of a problem if tying wings for sedges and the like.

If you do want to use synthetic sheeting for up-winged flies then keep it as a folded wing with the fold facing forwards.

Above: Dubbing material.

THE ART OF DUBBING

The secret of all dubbings is to use them sparingly. With soft underfur, the stiffer guard hairs or mixed fibre dubbing, first tease the fibres out onto the tying table surface with your fingers before spinning them thinly onto the silk.

If you need a bulky body, do not attempt it in the one go but build up the shape in several layers.

The normal method for dubbing onto a thread is to spin or roll the dubbing fibres around the thread with the first finger and thumb moving in just the one direction. If you use the dubbing loop way, it is best to spread the fibres evenly along one arm of the loop before laying the other arm on top.

There is another way that involves both these styles and is done this way. Dub the thread with the fibres first and then form a loop which is then spun tight to produce a really nice dubbing brush.

Some tyers use the "noodle" dubbing technique much favoured by American dressers such as Dave Whitlock where the dubbing is placed onto the flat of the palm and worked into a taper by rolling it back and forth with the other palm.

This tapered noodle is then secured in at

its thinner end with the tying thread before both are wound together to form the body.

Whilst every fly dresser aims for neatness and exact imitation, it is a well accepted fact by experienced fly fishers that the more straggly and untidy the dubbing, the better the fly will perform.

Body materials

These can be silk, floss, chenille, wool, quills, herls, whole feather herl, close-trimmed hackle feathers, raffia, latex, synthetic tubes, contoured ribbons, and single strands of natural fibres such as moose mane or horse hair.

BODIES FROM STRIPPED QUILLS

Peacock herl is probably the most used source of material whenever a fly calls for a stripped quill body. There is a problem. The feather is delicate and always seems to snap as you scrape away the flue off the fibres to bare the quill.

Instead of scraping, you can use bleach, boiling water or one of those creams that ladies use to remove hair from their legs. I have tried them all and have come down in favour of an old-fashioned typewriter rubber or eraser that looks like a pencil. If you find that the other ways make the quill brittle, try my way. You will not be at all disappointed.

Condor quill is no longer available and so substitutes such as turkey wing primary feathers, especially the spiky bits, have to be used instead.

Quill bodied flies can also be formed from strips of quill peeled from a wing or tail feather. Nick the stem with a sharp knife near its tip and then peel the hard shiny skin off in a downwards direction. Scrape off any pith with your fingernail.

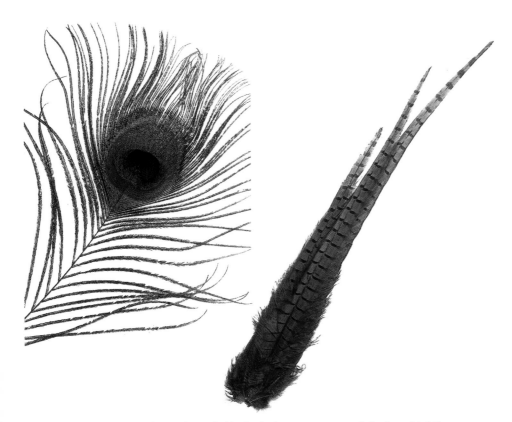

Above: Peacock eye plume (left). Cock pheasant centre tail feathers (right).

HERL BODIED FLIES

A very common way of making a fly body is to use the herls stripped from a feather such as a cock pheasant tail plume. These fibres are tied in by their tips and are then wound around the hook. Because they are quite fragile, it is wise to protect herl bodies with a wire or silk ribbing. Alternatively, wind it over a coat of fresh head cement.

Peacock and ostrich herls are used a lot too and both can be wound to form a body in several different ways.

Take a look at either feather really closely and you will see that the flue runs along one edge of the quill rather than down its centre. This unique feature can be used to make a very neat body if you take a single herl and then strip the flue from about half an inch at its thickest end. Tie this in at the hook bend so that the flue is at the rear of the herl. When carefully wound, the second turn of the herl will cover the exposed quill from the first turn and so on, giving a polished finish to the fly.

A tip about peacock herl. That taken from near the base of the feather is finer than that found close to the eye, so one peacock eye plume will provide all the quills you will need for a wide range of fly sizes.

Fly dressers are like magpies, their eyes being ever-alert to the potential of a scrap of material, fur or feather that might, just might, form the inspiration for that never-to-be-found ambition – the tying of the infallible fly sure to deceive trout wherever it is offered.

When hoarding away a material, we usually have a fairly good idea of how and where on a fly it will be used to best advantage. A particular kind of feather say, would be earmarked for the body of a fly to be fished at sedge time or perhaps a bit of fur put away for the time when attempting to imitate a certain insect in a specific stage of its development.

So, for the tidy-minded fly dresser whose precious collections of fur and feathers are carefully stored in easy to find groups, rather than the more usual jumble which resemble the fall-out following an explosion in a carpet factory, here's a brief run down on how certain materials should be used.

SILK

Spun and twisted silk has been used from the beginning of fly tying history. Some flies call for a bare silk body, while others have the silk covered with another material. Silk has been superseded by other man-made threads which are stronger, but there are still traditionalists who swear by silk and it is common to hear of old timers still referring to silk when they actually mean a modern thread.

FLOSS

Originally a heavier, un-twisted silk thread, floss is now more usually made from rayon, antron and various other synthetic fibres. Some flosses are supplied in a single strand, while others are bought in a double twist which is much easier to use if you untwist it before you start to tie the fly. Perfectly flat or tapered bodies resembling that of the insect being imitated, can be tied quite easily with floss silk.

CHENILLE

This is a plush pile yarn spun onto a fine thread core. It has a distinct nap and must, if the body is to look well, be tied in at the correct end. If it is not, the pile tends to pull out as the chenille is being wound

Opposite: Materials both natural and man-made.

onto the hook. Long a firm favourite with American, South African and New Zealand fly dressers, it has only really been used in English patterns for the last 30 years.

WOOL

Like silk, wool, is another historic fly dressing material. In early dressings, instructions to use 'crewel' as a body material abound, but it is little used today.

QUILL

The most commonly used form of quill is the fine quill taken from the magnificent peacock eye feather stripped of its fine flue. The tapered quills that come from the ordinary hackle feathers are also often used. One of the most unusual just has to be the quill peeled from the shaft of a chaffinch's tail feather.

HERLS

This really is a term given for any fibres torn or trimmed from a feather and then wound around the hook to form a body. Probably the most commonly used feathers are the long tail feathers from a cock pheasant or a peacock.

Whole feather herls are quite late-comers. This fairly new technique involves tying tiny, fluffy feathers in by their tips before being twisted into a rope and then wound on to form the body. The frond-like Cul de Canard plumes plucked from around a waterfowl's preen gland, top the list of feathers used in this useful way.

HACKLES

As well as being stripped as a quill, cock hackle feathers can be used with the fibres trimmed pretty close to the central stem. Flies using this more unusual body have built-in buoyancy and they look very natural too.

These long hairs are a useful alternative to stripped quill. Careful winding of the different coloured strands produce a segmented and life-like body.

Below: A top quality cock neck.

HORSE HAIR

The hair from the tail is stronger and more uniform in diameter and the most commonly used. These are not used a great deal these days, although flies and nymphs sporting horse hair bodies are beautifully translucent.

RAFFIA

Once used extensively for the bodies of mayfly imitations in Ireland and England is it has been superseded by other and more useful synthetic materials and latex in particular. The liquid latex is carefully spread onto glass and then rolled up as it dries to form little bodies which are then fastened onto the hook.

SYNTHETIC TUBES AND CONTOURED RIBBONS

This group gathers in everything from polythene stretched over the backs of nymphs and bugs to a whole host of synthetics which can be wound or even slipped over the hook itself to fashion the body. Some, such as Mylar are reflective while others like Larva Lace are translucent but most, if not all, are used in a fairly conventional manner and as substitutes for other body materials.

DUBBED BODIES

Dubbing is formed from the fur of animals from mice to bears and every other fur-jacketed creature in between. Fur comes in two main types – the soft downy underfur and the much stiffer guard or outer hairs.

A close look at a piece of rabbit fur still attached to the skin, reveals the differences well and this kind of fur is ideal for practice tying of dubbed bodies, it being quite easy after a while to pluck out each kind of hair separately.

Some furs are all soft like that owned by the mole. Some are spiky like that plucked from a hare's ear. A glance back through the old fly lists proves how long the different kinds have been specified for certain types of imitations or perhaps how they are best fished.

Today, most fly dressers prefer dubbings formed by mixing the soft underfur with the guard hairs.

One of the most popular dubbing furs was the fur taken from very young seal pups in the days when they were culled to protect high seas net fisheries. Seal fur has the ability to trap air in between the fibres making it just about perfect for nymphs and wet fly bodies, the tiny, glistening air bubbles giving the fly body a most natural and 'come and eat me' look.

Apart from old stocks, seal fur is very hard to find and the fur has been replaced by synthetic materials.

Some fibres, such as wool and un-spun silk normally used as wound bodies can also be used as dubbing materials, but they have to be chopped into tiny lengths first, teased out and then spun onto the thread.

BODIES FROM DEER HAIR

It was discovered many years ago that the hair on most kinds of deer is hollow and that when tightly bound, it flares and spins around a hook shank and there another important chapter in fly dressing history began.

Once spun onto the hook, the hollow and naturally buoyant hair is clipped to shape with sharp scissors or a razor blade. This technique is used to sculpt bodies and heads on a whole range of flies from those designed to ride the rapids through to fish imitations.

Because it is so buoyant, deer hair is often used to fashion detached bodies. Usually tied in by the tips, the hair is cross-wound with tying thread to the rear of the hook shank and then clipped to length. A bonus of the detached deer hair body is that a large fly can be tied onto a small hook, increasing the buoyancy factor while still retaining the fly's hooking powers.

Above: Deer hair.

All about hackles

The prime function of hackles is to imitate the legs and wings of the natural insect, or even the fins on fish-imitating lures.

Hackles are most commonly formed using small feathers. Tufts of wool or floss silk are used to a lesser degree.

They are most usually wound around the hook just behind the eye, but some patterns call for them to placed in a bunch under the fly's chin like a beard. Used this way they are called throat hackles. In a dry fly, the hackles serve two main purposes, that of supporting the fly on the surface as well as suggesting the tiny legs found on the natural insect.

Hackle feathers are taken from a variety of birds as well as from different parts of the plumage.

NECK HACKLES

The neck feathers from the domestic chicken are by far the most commonly used form of hackles. The cockerel feathers are used mainly for dry flies and some special wet flies and the softer ones from the hen almost exclusively for flies to be fished beneath the surface.

Of all the materials used by the trout fly dresser, probably the most desirable has been the top quality dry fly cock hackle feather and the search for those with hard, short fibres and natural dun colouring has been on for decades.

Even in the days of Halford and the traditional English style of dry fly, there was much debate about the shortage of good blue and honey dun hackle feathers suitable for small dry flies.

Today, modern genetic work has more or less solved the problem and many thousands of birds are reared with the fly dressers' needs in mind. While some are killed for their capes, some fowls are kept for years with two crops of hackle feathers being taken from them a year.

There are some famous names associated with this method of harvesting hackles, among them being the breeders of the Coq de Leon in Spain, French breeder and fly dresser Guy Plas and American Catskill tyers Reuben Cross and Harry Darbee who are reputed to have kept the 'cock of the moment' on a perch in the tying room and to have plucked the feathers they required for a fly as they needed them!

Apart from domestic fowls, hackles can be taken from almost any bird you can mention, although, most commonly used, are those plucked from either a partridge or a grouse.

RUMP HACKLES

Some of the Soft Hackle flies use the soft feathers from the rump area and should not really be confused with the special, oil-laden plumes found on ducks and other waterfowl. These are under feathers rather than plumage proper.

WING COVERTS

Many of the old patterns, especially the Soft Hackle clan, use feathers taken from either above or below the wing elbow and birds such as the brown owl, grouse and waterhen are much favoured. One of the most used covert feathers has to be the striking blue and black barred quill found on the English jay. Flies sporting these beautiful little feathers are much used in Ireland and on a host of flies intended for lake trout and sea trout.

BACK FEATHERS

Again, Soft Hackled flies are to the fore and perhaps the most used feather plucked from the bird's back has to be the speckled plume found on the English or Hungarian partridge. In addition to these soft-fibred feathers, certain flies are based on the feathers taken not from the neck, but the back of domestic fowl. These are very special fowls and probably the best known is the famed Coq de Leon from Northern Spain. These rare feathers are extremely long-fibred and are used in a particular way on both wet and dry flies.

HAIR HACKLES

Both fur and hair can be used as hackles as well as the more usual feathers. Typical examples are the internationally favoured Gold Ribbed Hare's Ear, the deer hair hackled dry flies and the ruff or collar on a muddler style lure.

HAIR ON THE SKIN

A more recent addition to the hair hackling techniques, this method uses rabbit, or similar fur, cut into narrow

strips across the grain of the pelt, tied in and wound like a hackle along the hook. The finished fly will be quite bulky but will have the distinct advantage of being highly mobile in the water.

Above: English partridge skin.
Next page: Capes and feathers of the highest quality.

Flies with wings

If the hunt through the centuries by fly dressers for the ultimate body material seems endless, then the search for the perfect wing must rival the quest for the Holy Grail. You name the fly dressing material and it has been used for a wing. Even the tiny see-through scales pulled from a pike's flank have been tried.

FEATHER WINGS

Wings can be formed by trimming small sections from a centre-tail feather or from feathers carefully selected to match each other for length, shape, colour and curve or by rolling a single section of feather which is then tied onto the hook either lying flat or upright.

BODY FEATHER WINGS

A less rigid wing is formed by using the finer-fibred feathers from mallard, teal, wood duck or even partridge in various ways. One is to use the whole feathers in the traditional fan-wing style. New Zealand fly dressers developed a couple of interesting styles using whole body feathers. One race of their flies have the whole feathers secured flat on top of the fly while another group, also firm favourites with South African fly fishers, have the feathers secured along the flanks of the fly.

Lastly we are back to the much in-vogue Cul de Canard feather which can be used either singly or in tiny, buoyant bunches.

THE HAIR WINGS

While European fly dressers have usually been first off the mark with new materials, there is little doubt at all that American and Canadian fly dressers were streets ahead when it came to using hair instead of feathers for fly wings.

The idea was in common use around the turn of the century and probably much earlier although it has not been recorded.

Once again, as with feathers, certain parts

Left: Mallard (left) and hen pheasant (right) wing quills.

Left: Moose mare tail.
Right: Squirrel tail.

of the bird or animal provide different textures of furs, each with a distinct use in both dry and wet flies.

TAIL HAIR

In most animals, the hair on the tail is usually the finest and longest, both desirable qualities for highly mobile and translucent wings. Bucktail and squirrel tails are obvious favourites.

BODY HAIR

Various kinds of deer provide the most commonly used hairs in this group. The bull elk or wapiti is a most useful animal for the fly dresser giving us hair, which although is not suitable for spinning around the hook, is just about perfect for forming wings.

HAIR ON THE SKIN

Instead of being trimmed off the skin, the pelt is trimmed with the grain into long and fine strips. It is then tied in fore and aft of the fly body like a mane. This style of tying features in many New Zealand and Australian fish-imitating lures and is now popular with fly fishers the world over. Rabbit and hare fur are used the most.

SYNTHETIC WINGS

The search for translucence has involved all manner of synthetic materials. Some have been used in sheet form, others as filaments and all with varying degrees of success. The simple flat sheet, while it has its obvious attractions, has never really caught on simply because the wings cause the fly to spin and twist in the air while it is being cast.

On the other hand, the filament forms such as the polypropylene yarns are much more angler-friendly and are much-used on all manner of flies from lures to nymphs and dry flies.

THE TAIL OF A FLY

Almost anything, from a bunch of fibres torn from a hackle feather through to a simple stub of wool, can be used as a fly tail. Recently, the term has been extended to include materials tied in to imitate the shuck discarded by the hatching insect.

Glossary

Terms used in fly dressing vary at times from country to country and sometimes have more than one meaning. Nevertheless, here's a brief list of those most commonly used.

FLIES

Attractor – a general term for non-imitative flies with a lot of colour or flash in their make-up.

Dry fly – one that sits on the surface film.

Emerger – a fly that sits in the surface film, part above and part below.

Lure – similar to the attractor but usually used to describe the larger flies.

Spider – mainly describes wet flies with sparse hackles and no wings.

Spent gnat – the dying female mayfly lying on the water after laying her eggs.

Spinner – a general term describing all flies dying after egg laying.

Tandem – a form of mount on which lures, streamers and bucktails are dressed to give extra length and which usually consists of two and sometimes three hooks joined one behind the other on a wire or nylon link.

Variant – a dry fly style with an extremely long-fibred hackle at least twice the normal length.

WINGS

Advanced wings – wings tied in so that the tips slope forwards. The hackles are wound behind the wings and are found mainly on dry flies.

Built or married wings – made up from slender slips from different wings and built up into a single, multi-coloured wing slip. Two matching slips are paired together for some wet flies. Not common on trout flies but a 19th century American fly, the Parma-chene Belle is a famed example.

Bunch wings – wings made up from bunches of feather fibre or hair. Used on both wet and dry flies.

Fan wings – dry fly wings made from a pair of duck breast feathers. Popular in the 19th and early 20th century mayfly patterns.

Loop wings – a fairly modern innovation where a wing is formed from fibres or fibres tied in by both butt and tip to form the loop.

Spent wings – usually hackle tip feathers, but sometimes bunches of hair of feather fibres dressed to lay flat on either side of the hook as opposed to being upright.

Streamer and bucktail wings – the former is made of feather and the latter hair. Both are very long wet fly wings.

Whole feather wings – wings made from a

pair of matched feathers. Usually found in traditional wet fly patterns.

Wonderwing – a wing formed from a feather that has had the fibres pulled downwards against the grain before being tied in as a whole feather wing. Used in a pair for normal dry flies, or singly on flat-winged sedge or stonefly patterns.

HACKLES

Beard hackle – a bunch of fibres tied in under the hook shank rather than wound around it in the usual way.

Collar hackle – a wound hackle put in front of a wet fly wing.

False hackle – the same as a beard hackle.

Parachute hackle – one that is wound around a projection tied at right angles to the shank so that the hackle lies horizontally. The projection can be a wire stub, a looped hackle stem, nylon loop or wing bunch.

Palmered hackle – one wound on open turns from front to back. Found on many dry and some wet flies.

Throat hackle – a hackle wound and then pulled down wholly below the shank and occasionally in front of a palmered hackle on a wet fly.

Umbrella hackle – a style that keeps popping up where the hackle is tied in and wound so that the natural curve sets the points forward with the best face of the feather facing to the rear. The forward tilt is increased by using turns of tying thread built up behind the hackle. The fly looks rather like an inverted umbrella and fishes with the hook perpendicular in the water. Originally popular as a dapping fly, the tying technique has appeared in various guises such as the Funnel Dun, a more modern dry fly that sports a tail which causes it to fish flat on the water with the hook point uppermost.

SPECIAL TECHNIQUES

Extended body – a fly body tied to extend beyond the hook bend, most often fashioned from deer hair but sometimes on a centre stem of stiff nylon. Older flies used bristles.

Detached body – almost the same but created as a separate unit and then tied on the hook shank. Can be made of deer hair, twisted poly yarn and even rubber latex smeared and rolled.

Dubbing loop – a loop of thread with dubbing laid between the two arms and then twisted by hand or with a special tool.

Packed hair – deer hair or similar to be trimmed to form a head or body as in a Muddler Minnow.

Pinch and Loop – an English term describing the method used when tying in materials such as wings. Soft, or Slack Loop is the term used in America.

Posting a wing – taking several turns around the base of a wing to reinforce it. Most frequently used on hair wings to make sure both of the wings are firm and well defined.

Stacked hair – hair of any kind used for a dry fly wing. Placed in a special stacker device and tapped to even up the hair tips before they are tied in.

FEATHER DESCRIPTIONS

Biots – the fibres from the narrow (leading) side of a primary feather. Used for some Stone Fly tails and antennae or wound to form a fly body.

Bow feather – not often heard. Refers to the covert feathers at the bend of a bird wing.

Covert – a small feather from near the top leading edge of a bird wing. Taken from the underside of the wing, it is known as an under-covert.

Hackle – unless otherwise stated, this is the neck feather, usually from a domestic cock or hen.

Saddle hackle – the long feathers that drape from the lower back of the cockerel. Usually finer in the stem than a neck hackle and with genetic improvements, of extreme length and supreme quality.

Spade hackle – from just in front of the saddle in between the wings. A short, spade shaped feather, it has fine, long fibres that make excellent tails and fibre wings. This is the feather used in the famed Coq de Leon patterns.

Swords – the side tails on a peacock, bright iridescent green used for flies such as Alexandra, and where a green herl is stipulated for the body as in the Red Tag, the ordinary peacock eye tail herl being a darker bronze/green.

Rump feathers – taken from the back of the bird immediately in front of the tail root. Found in the dressings of the Soft Hackle flies but most birds that provided the feathers used are now protected.

Tippet – used to describe the neck feather of pheasants, especially the Golden and Amhurst varieties.

Topping – the crest feather from the Golden or Amhurst pheasants. These Ruffed Pheasants are the only ones boasting a head plume. Both tippets and toppings are used for tailing traditional wet flies and less often for the wings.

GENERAL TERMS

Head cement or lacquer – Varnishes used to treat the head of a finished fly and to help 'glue' in difficult materials such as squirrel hair during the tying process. Available in clear as well as coloured. Nail varnishes, especially those mixed with nylon to strengthen nails are especially popular.

Hook eyes – blind eye, down or up eyed, ring or straight and loop describe the shape or place of the eye. By tradition, up-eyed hooks are used for dry flies whilst those with down-facing eyes are used for wets and this goes back to the days of stiff gut leaders and the special knots which would affect the way the fly sat on or in the water. Modern soft nylon and fine-wired down eyed hooks have almost superseded the old up-eyed dry fly hook.

The ring hook is not common and is used mainly in long-shanked versions for lures and streamers.

Forged – used to indicate that the bend of the hook has been struck whilst hot, slightly flattening the wire on each side to produce a stronger hook.

Below: Artificial fibres for use as tail whisks.

Index

Acknowledgments

Some of the flies described in this book originated in excess of a hundred years ago. They have withstood the test of time, technology, and "anglers myth" to remain as effective today as they have ever been.

For authenticity, the fly tying materials used are to the original and traditional recipes. These naturally occurring materials were originally chosen for their known behaviour and colouration when immersed in the water, and proven effectiveness over many years of subsequent use.

In certain countries, alternative or synthetic materials may be substituted if the original materials are not available, or are protected by law.

PHOTOGRAPHY

Chris Allen: Covers, End Papers, Pages - 1, 2, 3, 4, 6, 8-9, 11, 58, 60, 61, 64, 66 (BL), 69, 75, 76, 77, 78, 79, 81, 83, 84 and 88-89.

Russel Symons: Pages - 18, 20, 22, 24, 26, 28, 30, 32, 34, 36, 37, 42, 44, 46, 48, 50, 52, 53, 54, 56, 62, 63 and 66.

Coloursport - Ed Baxter: Pages - 7 and 59.

Optical Art - Simon Everett: Pages - 5 and 10.

Still Moving Picture Company - Doug Corrance: Pages 40-41.

Peter Gathercole: Page 13.

Advertising Archives: Pages - 9, 16 and 17.

ILLUSTRATIONS

Linden Artists - Jane Pickering, David Cook, Steve Lings.

Thank you to Mary White, Lathkill Tackle, for supplying equipment and materials for photography.

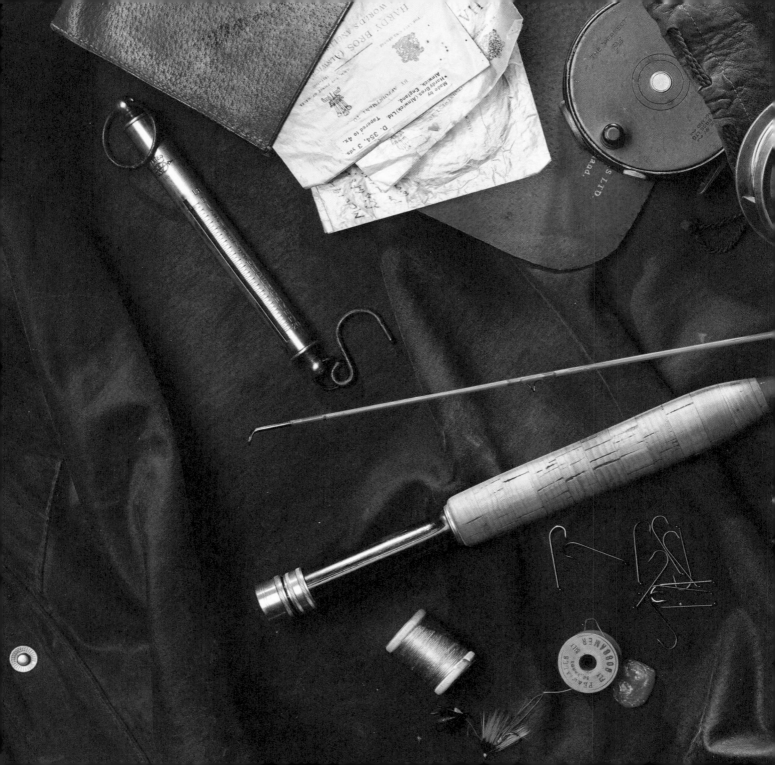